Short Bike Rides
in Eastern Pennsylvania

Short Bike Rides
in Eastern Pennsylvania

Second Edition

by Bill Simpson

An East Woods Book

The
Globe
Pequot
Press

Old Saybrook, Connecticut

Copyright © 1990, 1993 by William Simpson

Library of Congress Cataloging-in-Publication Data

Simpson, Bill, 1950–
  Short bike rides in eastern Pennsylvania / by Bill Simpson.—2nd ed.
      p.   cm.
  "An East Woods book."
  ISBN 1-56440-152-9
  1. Bicycle touring—Pennsylvania—Guidebooks. 2. Pennsylvania—Guide-
books. I. Title.
  GV1045.5.P4S56   1993
  796.6'09748—dc20   92-36026

Manufactured in the United States of America
Second Edition/First Printing

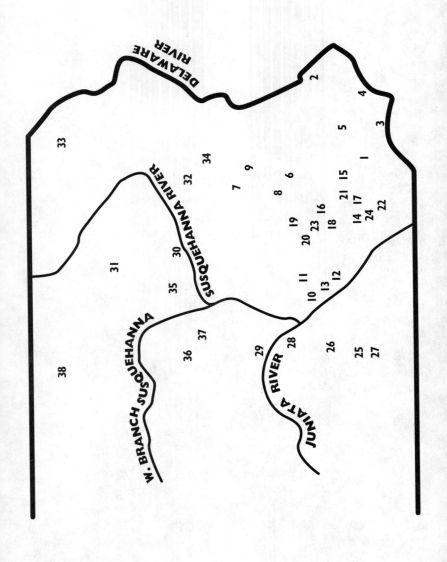

Contents

Ridge and Valley Region

Northeast

North Central

Introduction

Welcome to Pennsylvania. If your idea of the Keystone State is the cities of Philadelphia and Pittsburgh, you're in for a very nice surprise. Pennsylvania means "Penn's woods," and large areas of woodland still cover the state. Visitors to Pennsylvania , especially those from the West, are often amazed by the unending green — not money, but trees, grass, and crops. In the southeastern quarter of the state, where many of these rides take place, farming is the dominant industry. That means that there are plenty of back roads, and back roads mean nice riding.

Pennsylvania is a big state. That's why this book covers only the eastern half. Even so, it's well over 200 miles from Wellsboro, the northernmost ride, to Philadelphia, the southernmost ride.

The last time anyone checked, Pennsylvania had more roads than any other state in the country, although California was trying to pave its way into the lead. Lancaster County has more roads than any other county in the state. For that reason, Lancaster County is rumored to be one of the ten best places in the world for biking. Hundreds of miles of farm roads will earn a place that sort of reputation. This is one of the few areas where you can come to a covered bridge and encounter a traffic jam that consists of two bicycles and three horses and buggies.

Most of these rides go through rural areas. The exceptions are Philadelphia and Harrisburg, and these are both pretty rides. The Harrisburg ride follows the Susquehanna River, and the Philadelphia ride goes from the Schuylkill River to the Delaware.

In Pennsylvania you'll find varied attractions, ranging from historical sites such as Independence Hall and Wheatland, to battlefields at Gettysburg and Brandywine, to farms almost everywhere, to a wildlife preserve at Middle Creek, to a baseball team that plays in the middle of the river in Harrisburg, to the sweet smell of chocolate in Hershey and Lititz, to the Green Dragon Market in Ephrata, where you can buy almost anything that's ever been made.

These rides cover all sorts of terrain. The Hawk Mountain and

Jim Thorpe rides will challenge even the strongest riders. The Harrisburg and Washingtonville rides, on the other hand, are delightfully flat. Most of the others include a mix of hills and flat stretches. Some rides are largely sightseeing tours, and some are rides for the joy of riding, with minimal interference from cars. Several rides include a long and short option or an option to connect with another ride.

As you navigate your way through this region, it may be helpful to know that Pennsylvania has a two-tiered road-numbering system for state routes. When the route numbers are 999 or lower, large signs—about seven feet high—are used. These indicate a number only. When the route numbers are 1000 or higher, the signs are much smaller (only aboute three feet high). These carry a designation such as *SR 1006*, and because of their size, are easy to miss. All references throughout this guide to the "SR" routes carry the *SR* prefix. References to other state routes (999 or lower) are designated by the word *Route* only, for example, Route 34.

The book is set up to make your planning and riding as simple as possible. At the beginning of each ride description, you'll find these seven categories of information:

1. Distance of ride in miles
2. Approximate pedaling time
3. Description of terrain
4. Condition of the road surface
5. Things to see on the ride
6. Where you can find food on the ride
7. Locations of restroom facilities

The description of each ride tells you what to look for along the way, where to expect big hills, and the times of year when festivals and other events take place. The directions for the rides indicate mileage at each turn. These were checked on a bike odometer and should help guide you along the route.

Bicycling in Pennsylvania can be enjoyable and challenging. Enjoy, and ride safely.

Tips

Always wear a helmet.

Aside from cars, the biggest problem bikers face is dogs. Pennsylvania is no different from any other state in that respect. Especially in rural areas, people often let dogs run loose. Your best protection is some sort of spray. Tear gas carried in the back pocket of a biking shirt is ideal. It's easy to grab, and it will instantly stop Fido. But don't shoot into a strong wind.

The best times to ride are from about 9:00 A.M. to 2:00 P.M. Traffic is generally lightest then. And because many of these rides go to popular attractions, traffic is often lighter on weekdays than on weekends. Probably the best month for riding is October.

One of the most important safety devices to appear in many years has recently come out of southeastern Pennsylvania. The VistaLite's pulsating light makes riders visible in darkness, at distances up to 2,000 feet. Long before a driver is on top of you, he'll know that something is in the road ahead. The VistaLite is the creation of a Lancaster man, Robert Choi, and it's available in bike stores everywhere.

About the Amish

One factor that makes Lancaster and surrounding counties superb for bike riding is the Amish. The Amish are a people whose religious beliefs prohibit the use of such modern conveniences as electricity and cars. The Amish travel by horse and buggy. That creates some unusual, though very minor, road hazards. One is the ruts that the horses wear in the roads. Fortunately, the ruts are far enough from the edge of the road to leave plenty of room for a bike. The other hazard is what the locals call "road apples." These are what result when a horse has relieved himself on the road. Most riders are happy to navigate these obstacles in exchange for having the roads almost to themselves.

The Amish are friendly, but they value their privacy and will not consent to having their pictures taken. Please treat these people with respect.

The Weather

Pennsylvania's climate has some of everything. It can be seventy-five in January and freezing in April. But it's always hot in the summer. The driest months are generally September and October. In summer, rainy days are rather rare but thunderstorms are common. They usually pop up in the late afternoon or evening and generally roll in from the west.

It would be risky to plan a biking vacation for Pennsylvania in December, January, or February, but if you're coming during those months, it can't hurt to bring your bike. Every month has at least a few good days for biking, and the snow usually melts rather quickly. Local riders rarely endure more than two weeks when they can't do some riding.

Covered Bridges

As you pedal along on many of these rides, you'll come to covered bridges. There were once thousands of these structures in the state, but their number has dwindled tremendously. Today, approximately 230 remain in Pennsylvania. While many people associate covered bridges with Vermont, Pennsylvania has more than any other state.

Lancaster County has more covered bridges than any other county—thirty. One ride—Lancaster County Covered Bridges—takes you through five of them.

Southeastern Pennsylvania can rightfully claim to be the covered-bridge capital of the nation. The first one built in the country spanned the Schuylkill in Philadelphia. The longest one ever built—5,690 feet—crossed the Susquehanna between Columbia and Wrightsville.

Riding through covered bridges requires caution. It is possible to catch a tire between the boards, so it's a good idea to walk your bike through. It's also a good idea to make sure that there are no cars in the bridge when you cross. The bridges are fairly narrow, and it's difficult for the eyes to adjust from light to dark.

You can see covered bridges on these rides:

Blue Ball, Ephrata, Intercourse, Lancaster County Covered Bridges, Quarryville, Thompsontown, Bloomsburg, and Loganton. On the third Sunday of August, the Lancaster Bicycle Club sponsors its Covered Bridge Metric Century. This is a non-competitive, 100-kilometer ride which goes through seven covered bridges, and usually attracts more than 1,500 riders. Most of the ride goes through Amish farmlands, and the club provides food and sag wagons. If you'd like more information, call the club's hotline at 717–656–8744 for a recorded message.

Here are some facts on the covered bridges on the rides:

Ride	Bridge Name	Width	Stream	Year Built
Bloomsburg	Rupert	185'	Fishing Creek	1847
Blue Ball	Weaver Mill	88'	Conestoga River	1879
Ephrata	Rettew Mill	77'	Cocalico Creek	1891
Intercourse	Leaman Place	118'	Pequea Creek	1894
Lancaster Co*	Samuel Erb's	80'	Hammer Creek	1887
Lancaster Co	Rosehill	89'	Cocalico Creek	1849
Lancaster Co	Eberly's Mill	99'	Conestoga River	1846
Lancaster Co	Pinetown	133'	Conestoga River	1867
Lancaster Co	Hunsecker's	180'	Conestoga River	1975**
Loganton	Logan's Mill	63'	Big Fishing Creek	1874
Quarryville	Jackson's Mill	142'	Octorara Creek	1878
Thompsontown	Lehman/Port Royal	120'	Licking Creek	1888

* Bridges on Lancaster County Covered Bridges ride are listed in order they appear on the ride.
**Hurricane Agnes washed away the original Hunsecker Bridge, built in 1843.

Pennsylvania's Topography and Roads

Few people with a casual knowledge of the state would associate mountains with Pennsylvania, but Pennsylvania *is* a mountain state. If you look at a map, you'll see the word *mountain* all over

the place. The one exception is the southeast corner of the state. East and south of Harrisburg, it's comparatively flat, but it's still not like central Illinois. As a result, most of these rides take the rider over some hills. Because of the terrain, Pennsylvania's roads are rarely straight. They bend to follow a creek or to avoid a mountain.

To help you choose rides that are comfortable for you, here's the author's rating of the hilliest and the flattest rides:

Hilliest: Hawk Mountain, Jim Thorpe, Eagles Mere
Flattest: Harrisburg, Washingtonville, Hershey, Loganton, Bird-in-Hand, Thompsontown.

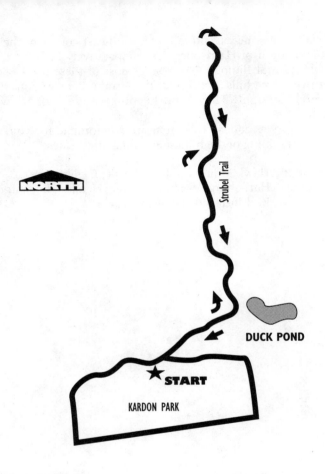

NORTH

Strubel Trail

DUCK POND

★ START

KARDON PARK

HOW to get there
Take Business Route 30 into downtown Downingtown. From the intersection of PA 282 and Route 30, go one block north on Green Street. Then go right on Pennsylvania Avenue. Kardon Park is on the left.

Downingtown

Number of miles: 6.2
Approximate pedaling time: ¹/₂ hour
Terrain: Absolutely flat
Surface: Fair
Things to see: Duck pond, shaded trail
Facilities: In park at beginning of trail

Pennsylvania has only a few biking trails. The Strubel Biking/Hiking Trail is a nice one. It's short and isn't suitable for fast riding, but it's an excellent place for parents and children to ride together and for children to learn to ride.

The trail, which utilizes an abandoned railroad right-of-way, is flat. A single-speed bike will work quite well here. The Brandywine Creek runs beside the trail, and tall trees line most of the route.

Since the trail is used by both hikers and bikers, it's important to be courteous to pedestrians, who usually outnumber bikers. Frequently, parents walk or run while their small children ride alongside.

Downingtown is a small, quiet town located on the outer reaches of the Philadelphia metropolitan area. The trail begins at Kardon Park, where a small pond is home to many ducks.

DIRECTIONS for the ride

- The Strubel Trail begins in Kardon Park and runs north, along the Brandywine Creek, for 3.1 miles.

Doylestown/New Hope

Number of miles:	30
Approximate pedaling time:	2½ hours
Terrain:	Flat to gently rolling
Surface:	Good
Things to see:	Mercer Museum, Michener Arts Center, Bucks County Playhouse, mule barge
Food:	In Doylestown and New Hope
Facilities:	In Doylestown and New Hope

Doylestown and New Hope are full of historic sites. Between them are miles of farm country and lightly traveled roads.

At the start of the ride are the James Michener Arts Center and the Mercer Museum. Famous writer James Michener grew up in Doylestown and has kept a home in Bucks County throughout his career. This Arts Center exhibits many pieces from his collection. The Mercer Museum holds what is considered to be the most extensive collection of Early American tools found anywhere. The May Folk Fest features local crafts and music.

The return trip passes the Moravian Pottery and Tile Works, housed in the building that Dr. Henry Chapman Mercer used for the production of pottery and tile. The Moravians belong to a Protestant sect that had its beginnings in the 15th century in Moravia, a region in what is now Czechoslovakia. They believe in the sole authority of the Bible and favor disciplined Christian living. The northern center of the Moravian Church is in Bethlehem, Pennsylvania, and Lititz, Pennsylvania, is home to a large Moravian congregation.

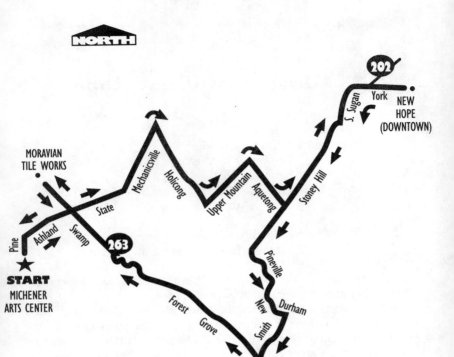

NORTH

MORAVIAN
TILE WORKS

Mechanicsville

Holicong

Upper Mountain

Aquetong

Stoney Hill

S. Sugan

York

NEW
HOPE
(DOWNTOWN)

202

State

Ashland

Swamp

Pine

★
START
MICHENER
ARTS CENTER

263

Forest

Grove

Smith

New

Durham

Pineville

HOW
to get
there
   Take the Pennsylvania Turnpike to the
Willow Grove exit and go north on Route
611. Take Route 611 to Main Street. The ride
starts at the Michener Arts Center and Mercer
Museum on Pine Street, just east of Main. Signs
will direct you.

 **DIREC- TIONS** for the ride

- Leave the Michener Arts Center parking lot and go right on Pine Street.
- Right onto Ashland Street at 0.1 mile.
- Left onto Mechanicsville Road at 1.7 miles.
- Right onto Holicong Road at 4.6 miles.
- Left onto Upper Mountain Road (no mountain) at 6.9 miles.
- Right onto Aquetong Road at 9.3 miles.
- Left onto Stoney Hill Road at 10.9 miles.
- Left onto South Sugan Road at 12.6 miles.
- Right onto York Road at traffic light.
- Straight at bend in road at 13.6 miles.
- After you ride (or park your bike and walk) around New Hope, return to this spot to return to Doylestown.

Return

- Merge onto York Road (U.S. 202), headed south.
- Left onto South Sugan Road at 0.7 mile.
- Right onto Stoney Hill Road at 1.7 miles.
- Left onto Pineville Road at 5.0 miles.
- Right onto New Road at 6.7 miles.
- Left onto Durham Road at 7.2 miles.
- Right onto Smith Road at 7.3 miles.
- Right onto Forest Grove Road at 8.4 miles.
- Right onto Route 263 north at 11.9 miles.
- Left onto Swamp Road at 12.2 miles.
- Turn around at Moravian Pottery and Tile Works at 14.7 miles.
- Right onto State Street (U.S. 202) at 15.6 miles.
- Left onto Ashland at 16.1 miles.
- Left onto Pine Street at 16.7 miles to finish.

The fine pottery you will find here is reflective of the strong Moravian work ethic and the pride they take in their crafts. Today, the museum in the restored building still produces tiles in accordance with Mercer's original methods. Leaving the pottery, be careful on York Road (Route 202). It's the busiest stretch of road on the ride.

As you leave Doylestown, you'll soon get onto country roads. Keep your eyes open for deer; they're pretty common in the area.

New Hope is an artsy sort of town. The Bucks County Playhouse is in a 200-year-old mill and stages Broadway productions from April through December. The streets are lined with antiques shops and small restaurants. The mule barge will take you on a trip down the Delaware Canal. It's good to park the bikes and take a walk. If you cross the bridge over the river, you'll be in New Jersey.

Longwood

Number of miles: 16
Approximate pedaling time: 1¾ hours
Terrain: Rolling
Surface: Good
Things to see: Longwood Gardens, Phillips Mush-room Museum, Brandywine River Museum, Brandywine Battlefield
Food: Stores and restaurants on U.S. Route 1 between Brandywine River Museum and Battlefield
Facilities: At Tourist Information Center, Museum, and Battlefield

This is an area rich in history, in horticulture, and even in wildlife. Although it's not a wilderness by any means, deer seem to love it and are almost as common as squirrels and robins. Most of the homes in the area are rather large, and most have substantial lawn and wooded areas around them.

The major attractions in the area are along U.S. Route 1. Although this is a busy highway, it's a model of what a highway should be. In most places, it has a wide shoulder that allows bikes and cars to coexist peacefully.

The ride begins at Longwood Gardens, at the Brandywine Valley Tourist Information Center. This restored building was a nineteenth-century Quaker meetinghouse. Many famous abolitionists spoke here before the Civil War. The center offers all sorts of information about the area.

The first point of interest on the tour is the Mushroom Museum.

NORTH

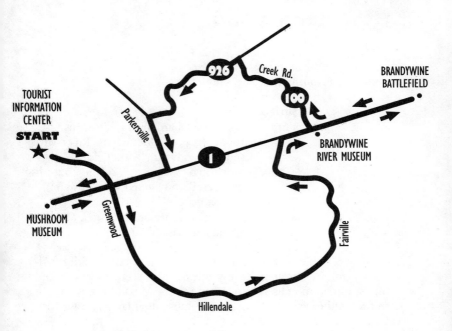

TOURIST
INFORMATION
CENTER
START

MUSHROOM
MUSEUM

Parkersville

926 Creek Rd.

100

Greenwood

Hillendale

Fairville

BRANDYWINE
BATTLEFIELD

BRANDYWINE
RIVER MUSEUM

HOW
to get
there   The ride begins at the Brandywine
Valley Tourist Information Center on
the grounds of Longwood Gardens, at the
intersection of U.S. Route 1 and Route 52.
There are good signs to direct you.

- From the Tourist Information Center, go right on U.S. Route 1.
- At Phillips Mushroom Museum, cross Route 1 (be careful) and revere your course.
- Right on Greenwood Road at 0.7 miles.
- Left on Hillendale Road at 2.0 miles.
- Merge into Fairville Road at 5.1 miles.
- Right onto U.S .1 at 6 .0 miles.
- Right into Brandywine River Museum at 6.2 miles.
- Back onto Route 1 and right.
- Left to Brandywine Battlefield State Park at 7.3 miles.
- Back onto Route 1 and right.
- Right onto Creek Road (Route 100) at 8.3 miles (traffic light).
- Left onto Route 926 at 11.4 miles.
- Left onto Parkersville Road at 13.2 miles.
- Right onto U.S .1 at 13.5 miles.
- Right into Longwood Gardens at 16.0 miles.

Nearby Kennett Square bills itself as the world's mushroom capital. In the museum you can learn all about the famous fungi, and in the gift shop you can buy many different varieties of mushroom straight from the farm. Mushroom farms, however, are different from other farms. Mushrooms grow in dark buildings, so don't look for any fields of fungi while you're riding.

After the mushrooms, about 5 miles of back roads wander through horse country. The next major point of interest is the Brandywine River Museum. Wyeth is the important name here. The museum frequently displays paintings and illustrations by Andrew Wyeth and other artists. Gardens of native wildflowers surround the museum.

A mile down Route 1 is the Brandywine Battlefield State Park, where one of the largest battles of the Revolution took place. Two farmhouses are on the grounds. One served as Washington's head-quarters and one as Lafayette's.

17

From here, it's onto country roads for a while, then back to Longwood and the 350-acre Longwood Gardens, one of the world's most amazing horticultural displays. Flowers, spectacular fountains, exotics, and native plants combine to create stunning effects. There are even illuminated displays choreographed to music.

Philadelphia

Number of miles:	12, 17, or 25
Approximate pedaling time:	$1/2$ hour to 3 hours
Terrain:	Flat, unless you go looking for hills
Surface:	Good
Things to see:	Museum of Art, Liberty Bell, Independence Hall, Memorial Hall, Fairmount Park, Penn's Landing, Academy of Natural Sciences, Boathouse Row, Mann Music Center, and much more
Food:	Many places on ride
Facilities:	At Fairmount Park, Independence Hall, and many other places
Options:	Ride up the Manayunk Wall (5 miles); ride through Center City (8 miles)

As the biggest city in the state and the "birthplace of liberty," Philadelphia offers many interesting attractions. It also has plenty of traffic; so much, in fact, that radio stations give traffic reports at midnight. Thus, this is more of a guide than a strictly planned ride. The best time to ride in Philadelphia is on a Sunday morning; next best is a Sunday afternoon.

Fairmount Park is a great place to ride. It's green—you'll even find raspberries and mulberries growing wild—and there are a lot of ducks and geese living here. If you stand on Kelly Drive and look across the river, you can almost imagine that you're in a wilderness. Trees and water are just about all that you can see.

The Museum of Art, where the ride begins, is the place where Rocky ran up the steps. It's home to collections ranging from Renais-

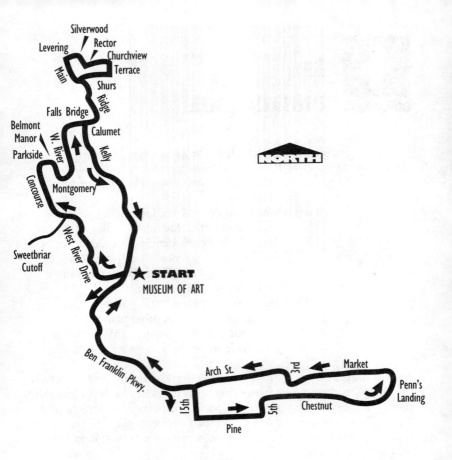

Silverwood
Rector
Levering
Churchview
Terrace
Main
Shurs
Ridge
Falls Bridge
Belmont
Manor
W. River
Calumet
Parkside
Kelly
Concourse
Montgomery
West River Drive
Sweetbriar
Cutoff
★ START
MUSEUM OF ART

NORTH

Ben Franklin Pkwy.
Arch St.
3rd
Market
Penn's
Landing
15th
5th
Chestnut
Pine

HOW
to get
there

The ride starts at the Philadelphia Museum
of Art. The Museum is beside the Schuylkill
River, close to the Schuylkill Expressway
(Interstate 76, which runs east and west). Exit the
Expressway at 30th Street and follow the signs.
Coming from the north or south, take Interstate 95 to the
Vine Street Expressway and go west. Look for signs for Ben
Franklin Parkway, which ends at the Museum.

DIREC-TIONS for the ride

- Start at Museum of Art and go north on West River Drive.
- Left at Sweetbriar Cutoff at 1.5 miles.
- Right onto Concourse Drive at 1.6 miles.
- Through big arches and straight to Mann Music Center.
- Road turns into Belmont Manor.
- Left onto Montgomery Drive at 5.0 miles.
- Left onto West River Drive at 5.4 miles.
- Right onto Falls Bridge Road at 7.3 miles.
- Right onto Kelly Drive (former East River Drive) at 7.5 miles.
- Return to Art Museum at 12 miles.

Manayunk Wall Option

- At end of bridge at 7.3 miles (Falls Bridge Road), straight onto Calumet Street.
- Left onto Ridge Avenue.
- Bear left onto Main Street.
- Right onto Levering Street.
- Right onto Silverwood Street.
- Left onto Rector Street.
- Straight onto Churchview Street.
- Right onto Terrace Street.
- Right onto Shurs Lane.
- Left onto Main Street.
- Right onto Kelly Drive (former East River Drive) back to Art Museum.

Center City Ride Option

- From Art Museum, go east on Ben Franklin Parkway.
- Left onto Arch Street.
- Right onto 15th Street.
- Left onto Pine Street.
- Left onto 5th Street (Independence Park is at Chestnut and 5th streets).
- Right onto Chestnut Street to Penn's Landing.

- West on Market Street.
- Right onto 3rd Street.
- Left onto Arch Street.
- Right onto Ben Franklin Parkway to Art Museum.

---

sance paintings to ancient Chinese works. The museum is right on the edge of Fairmount Park, and many local riders flock to this area. On Kelly Drive (formerly East River Drive) and West River Drive, there are paths for biking and running. These are in pretty good shape and let you ride without fighting the cars.

Begin at the Art Museum and head west on West River Drive. You'll be riding beside the Schuylkill River. At the Sweetbriar cutoff at 1.5 miles, turn left; then turn right at the stop sign. This will put you on Concourse Drive and take you through Fairmount Park. You'll pass Memorial Hall, which was built for the Centennial Exposition in 1876. Go straight ahead and you'll pass the Mann Music Center. This is home to summer concerts. The road changes names but just follow it. Eventually, it will become Belmont Manor Road. You'll see many horticultural exhibits in the park. When you come to a T intersection at 5.0 miles, make a left and go downhill. This will take you back to West River Drive.

Go left on West River Drive for about 2 miles. You'll come to Falls Bridge Road and a green metal bridge across the river. When you reach the other side, you'll have two options. If you go right, you can go back to the museum. If you'd like to ride up the Manayunk Wall, go left on Ridge Avenue. The Manayunk Wall is the toughest hill of the CoreStates Classic, a 156-mile bike race for the pros that's held here in June. To get to the wall, stay on Ridge Avenue for about a mile and a half. You'll come to an intersection where Ridge goes to the right and Main Street to the left. Take Main Street and go to Levering Street. Make a right and you'll be on "The Wall." It's a good hill, though not the toughest in Pennsylvania.

Back on Kelly Drive, you'll come to Boathouse Row. This is home to many rowing clubs, and on most days you can see rowers out on the river. At night, the houses are all lit up and make a striking sight, especially from the other side of the river. The Philadelphia Distance Run, a half marathon that attracts some of running's big names, is held on Kelly Drive and West River Drive on the third Sunday in September. Other bike races and running races take place here throughout the year.

You'll then come back to the Art Museum. If you wish to ride to such attractions as the Liberty Bell and Independence Hall, go in front of the museum, around the circle, and pick up Ben Franklin Parkway. This will take you into Center City. If you do choose to ride into Center City, expect to do battle with cars and trucks. When you reach the end of the Parkway, you'll be forced onto Arch Street. Here, you'll see signs for Tourist Information. Stopping here can be a good idea. They can give you information on what's going on at the moment and help you to plot your course.

To get to the Liberty Bell, go right on 15th Street and go down to Pine. Then go left on Pine and left on 5th Street. The Liberty Bell and Independence Hall are in the area around 5th and Chestnut. (If you'd like to see Veterans' Stadium, home of the Phillies and Eagles, turn right from Pine onto Broad Street. Broad Street would be 14th Street if it were numbered. The stadium is about 3 miles to the south.)

To get to Penn's Landing, the waterfront area along the Delaware River, return here and head east on Chestnut Street. Go as far east as you can. When you reach the river, you'll find shops, a museum, ships, and eating establishments.

To return, take the Market Street overpass across Interstate 95. Go to 3rd Street and go right. Then go left on Arch Street. This will take you through Chinatown and back to the Ben Franklin Parkway, which will take you back to the Art Museum.

If traffic doesn't bother you, Philadelphia's a great place to ride. If you don't care for traffic, it's still a good ride if you time it properly.

Valley Forge

Number of miles:	6
Approximate pedaling time:	1 hour
Terrain:	Moderately hilly
Surface:	Very good
Things to see:	Valley Forge National Historical Park
Food:	Snack bar on grounds
Facilities:	At Visitor Center and several places throughout park

Valley Forge is one of the names forever associated with the American Revolution. It was here that George Washington and 12,000 troops staged a six-month encampment from December 1777 to June 1778. During that time they kept the British army holed up in Philadelphia. Two thousand American troops died from disease, lack of supplies, and the severe winter. Still, during those hard times, the American army was reorganized. When they broke camp, they were a highly trained and very efficient unit. In a very real sense, the events that took place at Valley Forge allowed the colonists to win the Revolutionary War.

Today Valley Forge Park is a peaceful oasis close to the sprawl of Philadelphia. Inside the park, all is serene. Joggers and bikers are everywhere, and the twentieth century's hectic pace doesn't intrude on the green fields.

The park has a trail for biking and hiking. You can also rent bikes here. Begin at the Visitor Center and the trail will take you to all of the important sites. The huts in which the soldiers lived are memorable; *primitive* is too kind a word for them. They're log cabins with single wooden slats that served as beds. Life was not terribly comfort-

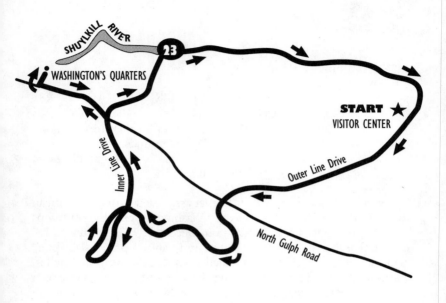

SHUYLKILL RIVER

WASHINGTON'S QUARTERS

23

START
VISITOR CENTER

Inner Line Drive

Outer Line Drive

North Gulph Road

HOW to get there Valley Forge is just northwest of Philadelphia. Take the Pennsylvania Turnpike to the Valley Forge exit (Exit 24). Take Route 422 west and follow the signs to the park. The Visitor Center is on the right as you enter the park.

- Begin at the Visitor Center.
- Go right, picking up bike/hike path along Outer Line Drive.
- Follow the bike path, in a roughly clockwise direction, through the park.
- To reach Washington's Headquarters, leave the bike path at about 4 miles and go left on North Gulph Road.
- Take second right (Inner Line Drive).
- Return to bike path and follow it back to Visitor Center.

able for the soldiers of the Revolution. The generals, of course, had more comfortable quarters. They used their rank to take over several local farmhouses.

If you come in June or July, you'll find wild raspberries growing in profusion along the roadsides. You can pick a lot and have a meal on the park picnic grounds.

This ride is short but very pleasant. The park is popular with local riders. It gives them an opportunity to get away from the heavy traffic on the roads outside the park. Despite the ride's shortness, you'll want to allow plenty of time to stop and play tourist.

French Creek

Number of miles:	19 or more. Exact distance will depend on riding done in French Creek Park. Distance between park and Daniel Boone Homestead is 9.5 miles.
Approximate pedaling time:	2½ hours
Terrain:	Hilly
Surface:	Mostly good; rough in French Creek Park
Things to see:	Daniel Boone Homestead, French Creek State Park
Food:	At French Creek State Park
Facilities:	At Boone Homestead and French Creek Park

This ride will take you over the back roads of eastern Berks County, through farmland and woodlands. Traffic is light and much of the route is shaded, so it's good for a hot day.

Daniel Boone was one of the great American frontiersmen. The Daniel Boone Homestead is maintained to show how Boone lived when he wasn't off exploring the wilds of the new nation. It also shows how the early English and German settlers in the area lived. On the grounds are Boone's house, a blacksmith shop, a barn, a sawmill, a Visitor Center, trails, and a picnic area.

When you leave the Homestead, you'll pass through farm country for several miles. There are several horse farms, and it's not uncommon to see people riding horses down the road. After you cross Route 422, the farms decrease and the land becomes wooded. You'll ride through the very small town of Monocacy. On Shed Road you'll go up an extremely long hill. Fortunately, it's not extremely steep.

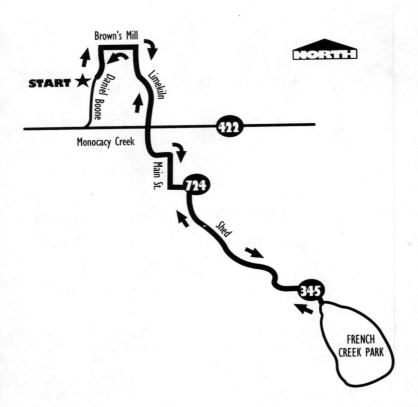

NORTH

Brown's Mill

START ★

Daniel Boone

Limekiln

422

Monocacy Creek

Main St.

724

Shed

345

FRENCH
CREEK PARK

HOW to get there — Take U.S. Route 422 east from Reading. Follow the signs to the Daniel Boone Homestead, which lies on Daniel Boone Road, just north of U.S. Route 422.

**DIREC-
TIONS
for the ride**

- Begin at Visitor Center at Daniel Boone Homestead and ride toward the entrance.
- Left on Daniel Boone Road at the entrance.
- Right on Brown's Mill Road at 1.5 miles.
- Right on Limekiln Road at 2.2 miles.
- Cross U.S. 422 at 4.4 miles onto Monocacy Creek Road.
- Right onto Main Street at 5.3 miles.
- Left onto Route 724 at 6.0 miles.
- Right onto Shed Road at 6.1 miles.
- Shed Road turns left at 6.6 miles.
- Left on Route 345 at 9.2 miles.
- Right into French Creek State Park at 9.4 miles.

Reverse

- Leave French Creek State Park and go left on Route 345.
- Right on Shed Road at 0.2 mile.
- Shed Road turns right at 2.8 miles
- Left onto Route 724 at 3.3 miles.
- Right onto Main Street (no sign) at 3.4 miles.
- Left onto Monocacy Creek Road at 4.1 miles.
- Cross 422 onto Limekiln Road at 4.9 miles.
- Left onto Brown's Mill Road at 7.1 miles.
- Left onto Daniel Boone Road at 7.9 miles.
- Right into Daniel Boone Homestead at 8.7 miles.

Shed Road ends right at the entrance to French Creek State Park. Here you'll find swimming, boat rentals, trails, and food. You'll also see signs for Hopewell Furnace National Historic Site. The furnace, which operated from 1771 until 1883, produced pig iron, hollowware stoves, and many other items. Many of the structures have been restored, and there are daily demonstrations of metal making during the summer. A Visitor Center has displays and examples of the tools used here and the pieces cast in the furnace.

The best part of the ride back is that you can go down the hill that you had to go up before.

NO TRESPASSING
BUFFALO HERD

Hawk Mountain

Number of miles:	10
Approximate pedaling time:	1 hour
Terrain:	Rolling to incredibly steep
Surface:	Good
Things to see:	Hawk Mountain, birds of prey, buffalo herd, butterflies, lush green valley, and Drehersville craft shops
Food:	Drehersville Country Store, at bottom of mountain
Facilities:	At Visitor Center on Hawk Mountain

This is a ride that will challenge the toughest hill climber. Although the distance is only 10 miles, the difficulty ranks with much longer jaunts. Fortunately the sights and the views make all the effort worthwhile. If you have a bike with granny gears, bring it. And bring your walking shoes. To enjoy this outing fully, you should take a short hike, and biking shoes are not suitable for the trail.

Hawk Mountain Sanctuary was established in 1934 to protect birds of prey. (Prior to 1934 shooters slaughtered the birds by the thousands.) From the top of the mountain you can watch the birds as they catch thermal updrafts and soar on the wind. The best time to take this ride is in autumn. During September, October, and November, an average of 24,000 raptors of fourteen different species pass over Hawk Mountain. Bald eagles and hawks come in September and October. Golden eagles come in November.

At the top of the mountain are a parking area and Visitor Center. Begin your ride at the Center. Walk your bike to the road, turn left, and head down the mountain. For about a mile and three-quarters, you'll have a free ride. At the bottom of the mountain is the tiny town

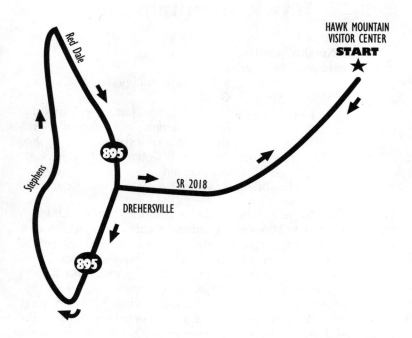

HAWK MOUNTAIN
VISITOR CENTER
START

Red Dale

Stephens

895

895

SR 2018

DREHERSVILLE

HOW to get there — Take Interstate 78 or U.S. Route 61 north. Follow 61 north to Route 895 east and look for signs to Hawk Mountain.

DIRECTIONS for the ride

- Left out of Hawk Mountain Visitor Center onto SR 2018.
- Left on Route 895 West at 2.0 miles.
- Right on Stephens Road at 2.8 miles.
- Right on Red Dale Road at 5.2 miles.
- Right on 895 West at 6.8 miles.
- Left on SR 2018 at 7.5 miles.
- Right to Visitor Center.

of Drehersville. Here you'll find the Drehersville Country Store and several stores selling locally made crafts and dolls. The craft stores are usually open only on weekends. When you reach the stop sign, go left on Route 895 West. The traffic on this road is light but swift, so be alert. Go about three-quarters of a mile and turn right on Stephens Road. About a mile down this road, you'll be greeted by a sight that most people wouldn't expect in Pennsylvania: a buffalo herd. These are the same animals that once dominated the scenery in the American West and provided Indians with food and clothing. Today, buffalo are making something of a comeback; some people consider buffalo a better meat than beef, so a few farmers are raising buffalo instead of cattle. From the valley floor you can often see the birds flying up on the mountain. And in the valleys you can see huge swarms of butterflies of many different varieties. You'll also see smaller birds, such as finches and meadowlarks.

Go past the buffalo herd and the stop sign. Then turn right on Red Dale Road. At the intersection of Red Dale and Route 895 is a small horse-show arena. There's no set schedule for the shows, but your best bet for seeing one is a weekend. At the intersection with Route 895, go right on 895 West. You'll soon see the signs for Hawk Mountain and Drehersville. Turn left on SR 2018 and begin your climb.

Back at the top a great view is waiting for you. Take the trail to the North Overlook to see the valley where you were just riding—and get an idea of what a climbing feat you performed.

At the Visitor Center there are displays and information, and in the fall there are guided lectures along the trail.

8 Reading

Number of miles:	10
Approximate pedaling time:	1 hour
Terrain:	One very good hill, mostly flat otherwise
Surface:	Good
Things to see:	Pagoda, shopping outlets, Luden's Candy Company, spectacular view of city and valley
Food:	Many places on route
Facilities:	At start of ride and several places along way

If you were to play a word-association game, Reading would draw two distinctly different responses from two different groups of people. Mention Reading to serious shoppers and the response would be "Outlets!" Mention Reading to bikers or runners and the response would be "Pagoda Hill!" This ride takes you to both of the attractions that make Reading famous.

Beginning at Penn's Commons Park, you'll go up Pagoda Hill, actually Mount Penn. This is a good climb, steep enough to have switchbacks. In truth, though, it's not such a bad hill. The switchbacks provide some flat stretches on the climb. The road at the other end of the hill, by contrast, goes straight up and is much steeper. When you reach the 2.7-mile mark on the ride, you'll be done climbing.

As you climb, drawings of the Pagoda on the road will lead you up. If you enjoy riding up this hill, you might make a note that there's an annual series of biathlons in this area. The races are held in spring, summer, and autumn.

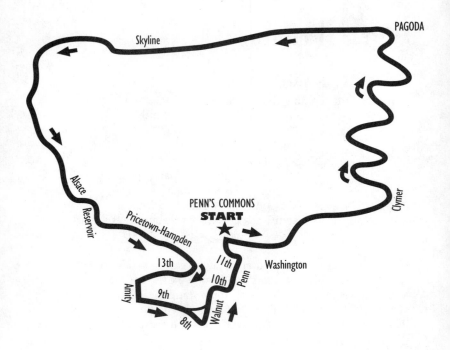

NORTH

PAGODA

Skyline

Clymer

Alsace

Reservoir

Pricetown-Hampden

PENN'S COMMONS
START

13th

11th

10th

Penn

Washington

Amity

9th

8th

Walnut

HOW to get there   Reading lies at the juncture of U.S. Route 222 and U.S. 422, midway between Allentown and Lancaster. Take the Pennsylvania Turnpike to the Lancaster/Reading exit and go north on 222. Penn's Commons park, the start of the ride, is close to downtown Reading, on Washington Street; turn east on Washington from Fifth Street, which is Route 222 and the main north/south road running through the city.

DIREC-TIONS
for the ride

- Begin at the red-brick bathroom in Penn's Commons and follow the road to your right, to the end of the park.
- Hard left onto Clymer Street at the upper end of the park.
- Follow switchbacks and painted PAGODA signs.
- Right onto Skyline Drive at 2.0 miles.
- Left at the end of Skyline Drive onto unmarked road at 4.5 miles.
- Right onto unmarked road (List Road) that goes down at 4.6 miles.
- Left onto Alsace Road at 5.1 miles.
- Right onto Reservoir Road at 5.3 miles.
- Left onto Pricetown Road at 5.5 miles.
- Pricetown becomes Hampden Boulevard.
- Make U turn onto Thirteenth Street at 7.0 miles.
- Left onto Amity Street at 7.5 miles.
- Left onto 9th Street at 7.9 miles.
- Merge into 8th Street at 8.4 miles.
- Left onto Walnut Street at 9.3 miles.
- Right onto 10th Street at 9.5 miles.
- Left onto Penn Street at 9.7 miles.
- Left onto 11th Street at 9.9 miles.
- Right on Washington Street and into Penn's Commons at 10.0 miles.

When you reach the top, you'll be on Skyline Drive and you'll enjoy an absolutely spectacular view of the city and valley below. The river that cuts through is the Schuylkill. It's heading to Philadelphia. It is interesting to see how much of the area is still forested. It appears that trees are still in control.

At the end of Skyline Drive, go left. You will quickly be faced with a choice of three roads. The one to the right goes up. The other two go down. Take the one in the middle.

At the bottom of the hill, you'll ride on some broad boulevards, and see some beautiful homes. Then you will arrive at Reading's outlets, where you can buy all sorts of merchandise at reduced prices.

People come from miles away to shop here. You can find clothing, food, shoes, and much more.

Just past the outlets is the Luden's Candy Company, famous for its cough drops and Fifth Avenue candy bars. After you pass Luden's, you'll go through a few blocks of the city, then back to Penn's Commons.

Trexlertown

Number of miles:	21
Approximate pedaling time:	1¾ hours
Terrain:	Hilly
Surface:	Good
Things to see:	Bike races at Lehigh County Velodrome; Rodale Research Center
Food:	Best to bring your own
Facilities:	At Velodrome and Research Center

This is a scenic, low-traffic, out-and-back ride that will give you an opportunity to ride in a way that you've probably never experienced before. You'll also have an opportunity to see food produced in a very unusual way.

Trexlertown is just south of Allentown. It is the home of the Lehigh County Velodrome, one of just a few bike-racing tracks in the United States. On Tuesday and Friday nights throughout the summer, riders from beginners to world champions race around the concrete oval. Track racing is not at all like road racing. The bikes have only one gear and no brakes. The riders spend much of their time jockeying for position. Then they sprint madly to the finish. The margin of victory is often less than a wheel.

If you'd like to give track riding a try, you're welcome to do so. The Velodrome is open to the public most of the time. Generally, the pros work out in the morning and evening; afternoons are best for amateurs. But be careful when you get on the track. It's steeply banked and it's impossible if it's wet. For a racing schedule, call the Velodrome at (215) 965–6930.

When you leave the Velodrome, you'll travel for 10½ miles through beautiful farmlands over the hills of Lehigh and Berks coun-

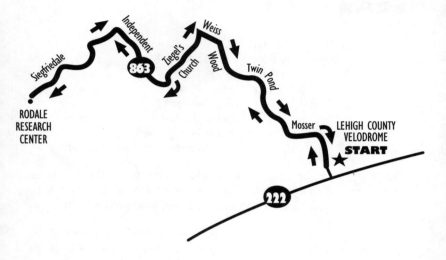

RODALE
RESEARCH
CENTER

863

222

LEHIGH COUNTY
VELODROME
START

HOW to get there Trexlertown is on U.S. Route 222, south of Allentown and north of Reading. The ride begins at the Velodrome, which is on 222, just south of the traffic light. Coming from the north, bear right on Mosser Road at a Mobil station. From the south, make a left on Mosser just after you pass Cycle Sports, the local bike shop.

DIREC-TIONS for the ride

- Leave Velodrome parking lot and go right on Mosser Road.
- Right onto Twin Pond Road at 1.4 miles.
- Right onto Wood Lane at 3.7 miles.
- Left onto Weiss Road at 4.4 miles.
- Left onto Ziegel's Church Road at 4.6 miles.
- Right onto Independent Road (Route 863 north) at 5.7 miles.
- Left onto Siegfriedale Road at 8.2 miles.
- Rodale Research Center at 10.5 miles.

Reverse

- Head back on Siegfriedale Road.
- Right on Independent Road (Route 863 south) at 2.1 miles.
- Left onto Ziegel's Church Road at 4.7 miles.
- Right onto Weiss Road at 5.7 miles.
- Right onto Wood Lane at 5.9 miles.
- Left onto Twin Pond Road at 6.6 miles.
- Left onto Mosser Road at 8.9 miles.
- Return to Velodrome at 10.5 miles.

ties. On Siegfriedale Road you will come to a little red schoolhouse. This is the Visitor Center and bookstore for the Rodale Research Center. The Rodale family publishes such magazines as *Prevention* and *Bicycling* in nearby Emmaus. On this research farm, they're exploring ways to produce foods without using harmful chemicals. If you take a tour of this farm, you'll see the food that looks perfect without the benefit of pesticides or herbicides. The apples shine as brilliantly as any sprayed with Alar.

One of the most interesting parts of the Rodale farm is the amaranth project. Amaranth is a hardy annual plant that's native to the Americas. It's drought resistant and high in protein, and it was an important food crop for the Aztecs. When amaranth is ripe, usually in August, the heads turn flaming red.

The people who work here are seriously involved in what they're doing, and they are happy to discuss their work.

Harrisburg

Number of miles:	15.5
Approximate pedaling time:	1½ hours
Terrain:	Flat
Surface:	Good
Things to see:	State Capitol, State Museum, Farm Show, Museum of Scientific Discovery, Harrisburg Senators baseball team, Harrisburg Marathon, Dauphin County Historical Society
Food:	All along the route
Facilities:	All along the route

Pennsylvania's capital city has many sights to see and offers a surprisingly nice city ride. Of course, it's best not to ride during morning or evening rush hour.

The first few miles are through an industrial area; although there's not a lot of traffic here, most of it is trucks. Still, it's a place favored by local bikers. After you leave the industrial area, you'll move onto Sixth Street, a broad boulevard, and then follow a designated bike route for a few miles. Front Street is a good place to try out your speed. It's straight and flat. It's best, however, not to exceed the posted speed limits. Below Front Street, at the water's edge, is a trail that's good for walking, running, and biking—except during floods.

The river is the Susquehanna. It's too shallow and rocky for shipping but it is wide. Upstream there are long stretches without a bridge. City Island, in the middle of the river, offers many recreational opportunities. The Harrisburg Senators minor league baseball team plays here, and the Harrisburg Marathon, held in November, finishes here.

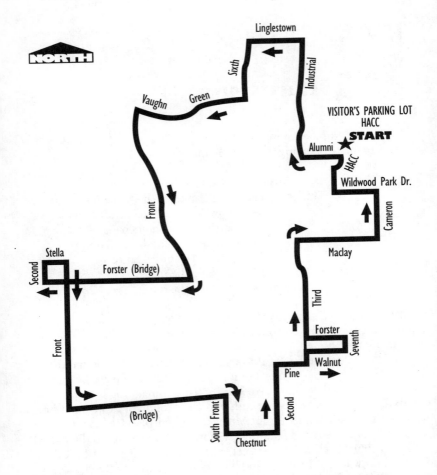

NORTH

Linglestown

Sixth

Industrial

Vaughn   Green

VISITOR'S PARKING LOT
HACC
START

Alumni

HACC

Wildwood Park Dr.

Front

Cameron

Stella

Forster (Bridge)

Maclay

Second

Third

Front

Forster

Seventh

Walnut

(Bridge)

Pine

South Front

Second

Chestnut

HOW
to get
there

Harrisburg is accessible by the Pennsylvania
Turnpike, Interstate 83, U.S. Route 322, and
U.S. Route 22. The ride begins at Harrisburg
Area Community College (HACC) on Cameron
Street, U.S. 22, just north of the Farm Show. An exit
from Interstate 81 is right there.

DIREC-TIONS for the ride

- Leave the HACC visitors parking lot and go left on Alumni Drive.
- Right onto Industrial Road at 0.1 mile.
- Left onto Linglestown Road at 2.5 miles.
- Left onto Sixth Street (sign for Bike Route).
- Right onto Green Street at 3.8 miles.
- Right onto Vaughn Street at 4.7 miles.
- Left onto Front Street at 4.9 miles.
- Right onto Forster Street at 7.6 miles.
- Cross the Susquehanna River.
- Right onto Second Street at 8.4 miles.
- Right onto Stella Avenue at 8.5 miles.
- Right onto Front Street (U.S. Routes 11 and 15) at 8.6 miles.
- Left onto bridge at 9.8 miles (sign: HARRISBURG 1).
- Right onto South Front Street at 10.6 miles.
- Left onto Chestnut Street at 10.7 miles.
- Left onto Second Street at 10.8 miles.
- Right onto Pine Street at 11.2 miles.
- Left onto Third Street at 11.3 miles.
- Right onto Forster Street at 11.4 miles.
- Right onto Seventh Street at 11.7 miles.
- Right onto Walnut Street at 12.1 miles.
- Right onto Third Street at 12.3 miles.
- Right onto Maclay Street at 13.7 miles.
- Left onto Cameron Street (U.S. Route 22) at 14.6 miles (Farm Show).
- Right onto Wildwood Park Drive at 15.0 miles.
- Left onto HACC Drive at 15.2 miles.
- Left onto Alumni Drive at 15.5 miles.

Back on solid ground, you'll see the State Capitol, an impressive edifice where Pennsylvania's legislators meet. Inside Strawberry Square, a shopping complex at Third and Walnut, is the Museum of Scientific Discovery. This is a hands-on science center with some fascinating displays. The State Museum, on Third between North and Forster, details the history of geology, science, industry, the military and much more in Pennsylvania.

Near the end of the ride, on Cameron Street, is the State Farm Show Building. The Farm Show is held every January, and snow always falls on Farm Show week. Other events such as Auto Shows and Home Builders Shows are also held here. There's even a Horse Show in October. In years past many basketball games were played here but the dusty arena never won great favor with fans or players.

Hershey

Number of miles:	10
Approximate pedaling time:	1½ hours
Terrain:	Rolling to flat
Surface:	Good
Things to see:	HersheyPark, Chocolate World, Founder's Hall, HersheyPark Arena
Food:	Everywhere
Facilities:	Numerous

The small town of Hershey has a big reputation for supplying the world with chocolate and with fun. The Hershey Bar is perhaps the most famous piece of candy in the world, and HersheyPark is Pennsylvania's version of Disneyland. This is a town where people come to enjoy themselves and to eat. The ride takes you to the major attractions in town. The street lights are shaped like Hershey Kisses, and the streets have names such as Chocolate Avenue and Cocoa Avenue. The prevailing aroma is that of chocolate.

The ride begins at the HersheyPark Visitor Center and takes you on a jaunt around town. Hershey is a developed area, but most of it remains green; in fact, there are still farms right in town. The reason is the Milton Hershey School. This school, founded by the man behind the chocolate company, cares for and educates children whose parents are unable to do so. It has some of the most impressive grounds and athletic facilities of any school anywhere.

On the school grounds is Founder's Hall, a monument to Milton and Catherine Hershey. It has a Visitor Center, a Heritage room, a banquet hall, and an auditorium. Tours are available.

Hershey Park offers more than forty rides and food of almost all

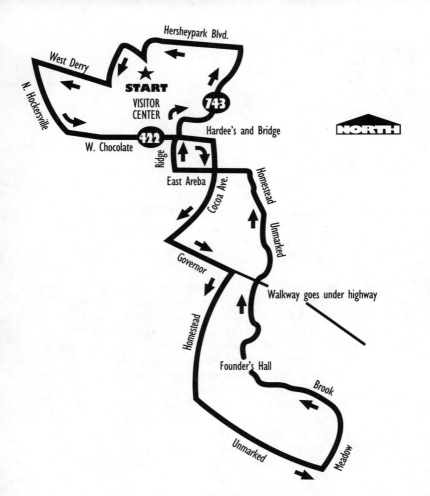

Hersheypark Blvd.

West Derry

N. Hockersville

START

VISITOR CENTER

743

Hardee's and Bridge

NORTH

422

W. Chocolate

Ridge

East Areba

Cocoa Ave.

Homestead

Unmarked

Governor

Walkway goes under highway

Homestead

Founder's Hall

Brook

Unmarked

Meadow

HOW to get there Hershey is about 10 miles east of Harrisburg. U.S. Routes 322 and 422 and Routes 743 and 39 go through town. The ride starts at the Visitor Center on Route 743.

- From Hershey Park Visitor Center, go right; follow EXIT signs. At stop sign, go left.
- Bear right onto West Derry Road at YIELD sign at 0.3 mile.
- Left on North Hockersville Road at 0.6 mile.
- Left on West Chocolate Avenue at 1.1 miles.
- Left onto main portion of U. S. Route 422 (West Chocolate Avenue) at 1.4 miles.
- Right onto Cocoa Avenue at 2.0 miles.
- Left onto Governor Road at 2.6 miles.
- Right onto Homestead Lane at 3.2 miles.
- Left at dead end (sign in middle of road) at 4.0 miles.
- Left onto Meadow Lane at 4.6 miles.
- Left onto Brook Drive at 5.2 miles.
- Bear right onto Homestead at 5.9 miles.
- Bear right to Founder's Hall at 6.3 miles.
- Circle in front of Founder's Hall and head back out.
- Right at bottom of little hill, onto walking trail at 6.5 miles.
- Left at pond, onto walkway that runs under highway.
- Right at first road after underpass.
- Left at stop sign at 7.2 miles.
- Right onto Homestead at 7.9 miles.
- Left onto East Areba Avenue at 8.1 miles.
- Right onto Ridge Avenue at 8.5 miles.
- Right and quick left under bridge at Hardee's at 8.7 miles.
- Right at stop sign after bridge.
- Left onto Route 743 at 9.0 miles.
- Left onto HersheyPark Boulevard at 9.5 miles.
- Left to Visitor Center at 10 miles.

known varieties. It has theaters with live entertainment, and from the Kissing Tower you can get a great view of the surrounding valley. Chocolate World will show you just how cacao beans and milk join forces to produce milk chocolate. HersheyPark Arena is home to the Hershey Bears minor league hockey team, and it hosts concerts and events such as professional wrestling. It was in this building that Wilt Chamberlain scored one hundred points in a game against New York in 1962.

Marietta

Number of miles:	14.7
Approximate pedaling time:	1½ hours
Terrain:	Rolling
Surface:	Good
Things to see:	Small towns and big houses, Cameron Estate Inn
Food:	Stores and restaurants in Marietta and Maytown
Facilities:	At park on East High Street in Maytown

A ride around Marietta will take you through several small towns, over country roads, and past plenty of farms. And this ride doesn't have any really steep hills; it's either gently rolling or flat.

In Marietta, as you ride down Market Street, you'll see a lot of magnificent homes. They're big and architecturally intriguing. Several even have stained-glass windows. In the center of town are the kinds of businesses that you'd expect to find in a small town—grocery stores, restaurants, and hardware stores.

As you leave Marietta, you go directly from town to the country. There really aren't any outskirts of this town. You'll ride past several farms, then into Maytown. This is a picturesque metropolis of perhaps a thousand. It has a beautiful little square with trees in the middle of the intersection. There are several businesses and a restaurant on the square.

Just east of the Maytown square, on East High Street, is a park where you can stop to refresh yourself. A few miles later, on Donegal Springs Road, you'll see the Donegal Witness Church and the Done-

53

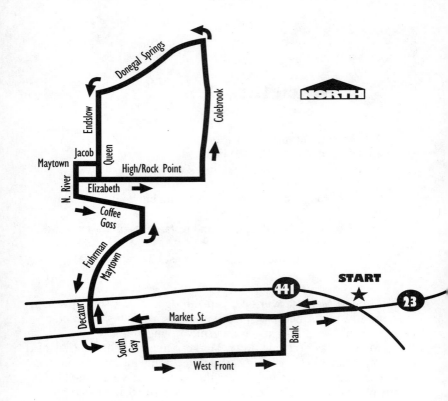

HOW to get there   Marietta lies at the intersection of Routes 23, 441, and 743, about 3 miles north of Columbia and U.S. Route 30. From Route 30, exit at 441 and go north. You can park on West Market Street, near the intersection of 23 and 441.

DIRECTIONS for the ride

- Go west on Market Street.
- Right onto Decatur Street at 1.8 miles.
- Cross Route 441 onto Maytown Road at 2.1 miles.
- Right onto Fuhrman Road at 2.4 miles.
- Left onto Coffee Goss Road at 2.9 miles.
- Bear right at church at 3.9 miles.
- Right onto Elizabeth Street at 4.0 miles.
- Left onto Queen Street at 4.1 miles.
- Left onto Jacob Street at 4.3 miles.
- Left onto North River Road at 4.4 miles.
- Left onto East High Street at 4.5 miles (town square).
- High Street becomes Rock Point Road.
- Left onto Colebrook Road at 6.2 miles.
- Left onto Donegal Springs Road at 7.9 miles.
- Left onto Endslow Road at 9.1 miles.
- Right onto Elizabeth Street at 10.5 miles.
- Left onto Coffee Goss Road at 10.6 miles.
- Right onto Fuhrman Road at 11.1 miles.
- Left onto Maytown Road at 12.1 miles.
- Cross Route 441 onto Decatur Street at 12.5 miles.
- Left onto Market Street at 12.7 miles.
- Right onto South Gay Street at 13.3 miles.
- Left onto West Front Street at 13.4 miles.
- Left at bank at 14.3 miles (no street sign).
- Right onto Market Street at 14.4 miles.
- Finish at 14.7 miles.

gal Witness Tree. This tree has been around for hundreds of years. You'll be able to identify it by its unusual girth. Next door to the Donegal Witness Church is the Cameron Estate Inn, a restored inn from the early 1800s. It now has guest rooms and a restaurant. Just past here is an airport; watch out for low-flying aircraft. When you return to Marietta, you'll turn onto Front Street. From this thoroughfare you can walk down to the Susquehanna River. There are several paved paths that cross the Conrail tracks and lead to the water. On Front Sreet you'll see antiques shops as well as neighborhood taverns. It's an interesting mix.

Three Mile Island

Number of miles:	19
Approximate pedaling time:	1½ hours
Terrain:	Moderately hilly
Surface:	Fair
Things to see:	Three Mile Island Nuclear Power Plant, Nissley Winery and Vineyards
Food:	Convenience store at intersection of River Road and Chestnut Street in Bainbridge
Facilities:	At TMI Visitor Center and Nissley Winery

On March 30, 1979, the eyes of the nation and the world focused on the Three Mile Island nuclear power plant in Pennsylvania, about 10 miles down the Susquehanna River from Harrisburg. Around 4:00 A.M., an "incident" occurred that threatened to lead to meltdown. Residents of the area headed out of town while officials assured them that all was well. For weeks, people lived on the brink. President Carter came to inspect the damage and to say that the crisis had passed. Fortunately, meltdown never occurred, and the area gradually returned to normal life.

Today the plant is back in operation, and the Visitor Center offers tours and educational displays and even computer games that test your knowledge of nuclear power. While the accent is on the positive aspects of nuclear power, there's no attempt to pretend that the accident never happened. Displays detail the entire chain of events.

The roads on the mainland near Three Mile Island are lightly traveled and ideal for biking. As you head away from the river, you'll

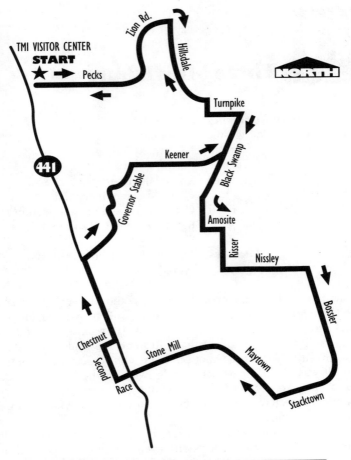

TMI VISITOR CENTER
START

Zion Rd.

Hillsdale

Pecks

NORTH

441

Turnpike

Keener

Black Swamp

Governor Stable

Amosite

Risser

Nissley

Bossler

Chestnut

Stone Mill

Second

Maytown

Race

Stacktown

HOW to get there
Three Mile Island is on Route 441, along the Susquehanna River, between Middletown and Marietta. From U.S. Route 30, exit at Columbia and go north on 441. From Route 283, exit on 441 and go south. Home base for the ride is the TMI Visitor Center.

- Leave the Three Mile Island Visitor Center and go right on Pecks Road.
- Left onto Zion Road at 0.5 mile.
- Right onto Hillsdale Road at 1.2 miles.
- Left onto Turnpike Road (T intersection, no sign) at 3.3 miles.
- Right onto Black Swamp Road at 3.6 miles.
- Left onto Amosite Road at 5.3 miles.
- Right onto Risser Road at 5.5 miles.
- Left onto Nissley Road (T intersection, no sign) at 6.1 miles.
- Right onto Bossler Road at 6.9 miles.
- Right onto Maytown Road (T intersection, no sign) at 9.3 miles.
- Left onto Stone Mill Road at 9.9 miles.
- Stone Mill Road becomes Race Street when you cross Route 441.
- Right onto Second Street in Bainbridge at 10.4 miles.
- Right onto Chestnut Street at 10.7 miles.
- Left onto Route 441 at 11.0 miles.
- Right onto Governor Stable Road at 12.6 miles.
- Right onto Keener Road at 13.6 miles.
- Left onto Black Swamp Road at 14.4 miles.
- Right onto Hillsdale Road at 15.5 miles.
- Left onto Zion Road at 17.5 miles.
- Right onto Pecks Road at 18.3 miles
- Left to Visitor Center

move into an area of farms and woods. Small streams wind their way slowly to the big river, and rabbits munch greenery by the side of the road.

On Maytown Road is the Nissley Winery, where you can watch all the steps involved in changing grapes into wine. The harvest takes place in late summer and fall. Bottling occurs in spring. Tours of the plant are available, and concerts and various special events take place on the grounds throughout the year. On the first Saturday in October, there's a 7-mile run. This event is famous among local runners, as the race in which a cow got loose and trotted along with the runners for several miles. She showed good speed, but her training had been for shorter distances.

The little town of Bainbridge is the only settlement that you'll pass through on the ride. This is a quiet place where you can stop for a cold drink and something to eat.

If you'd like to go right through TMI, your best opportunity comes on the third Saturday in September. That's when there's a 5-mile race called the Reactor Run-by. Three of the five miles are on the island.

Bird-In-Hand

Number of miles:	17
Approximate pedaling time:	1½ hours
Terrain:	Flat
Surface:	Fair; be careful of ruts worn by horses
Things to see:	Bird-In-Hand Farmer's Market, Mascot Roller Mill, Miller's Store, Amish farmlands
Food:	Farmer's Market, Kauffman's Store, Miller's Store; roadside produce stands
Facilities:	At Farmer's Market; outhouses at one-room schools on course

Bird-In-Hand is in the heart of Pennsylvania Dutch country. The area nearby is one of the world's most fertile agricultural regions; and it's also a great place for biking. The back roads are numerous and the traffic on them is light. In fact, much of the traffic consists of Amish horses and buggies, not cars.

Because the Amish are an agrarian society, most of the area's attractions center on food. At the Bird-In-Hand Farmer's Market, where the ride begins, you can find many familiar favorites and perhaps some local delicacies that aren't found everywhere else. In summer and fall, local produce is abundant.

As you begin the ride, you immediately enter farm country. You'll probably see some farmers working their fields with teams of draft horses. The Amish don't use modern equipment, but their farms are tremendously productive. Most of these farms are relatively small, and every member of the family pitches in.

On many of the farms, you'll see signs advertising nonfood items

61

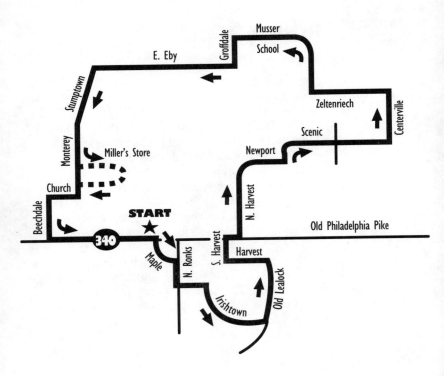

NORTH

Musser
School
E. Eby
Groffdale
Stumptown
Zeltenriech
Centerville
Monterey
Scenic
Miller's Store
Newport
Church
N. Harvest
Beechdale
START
Old Philadelphia Pike
340
Maple
N. Ronks
S. Harvest
Harvest
Old Leacock
Irishtown

HOW to get there   Take the Pennsylvania Turnpike to Lancaster/ Reading exit (Exit 21). Go south on U.S. 222. Go east on U.S. 30 and then east on Route 340 for about 5 miles until you reach the Bird-In-Hand Farmer's Market, where the ride starts. Or take U.S. 30 east of Lancaster to Route 896. Go north on Route 896 to Route 340. Then go east on Route 340 for about 3 miles to the Farmer's Market.

- Go to west end of Farmer's Market parking lot and go left on Maple Avenue.
- Right onto North Ronks Road at 0.4 mile.
- Left onto Irishtown Road at 0.7 mile.
- Left onto Old Leacock Road at 2.9 miles.
- Left onto Harvest /South Harvest Road at 3.7 miles.
- Right onto Old Philadelphia Pike at 5.5 miles.
- Left onto North Harvest Road at 5.6 miles.
- Straight through stop sign at 6.9 miles onto Newport Road.
- Left onto Scenic Road at 7.3 miles.
- Right and left, staying on Scenic, at 8.0 miles.
- Left onto Centerville Road at 8.7 miles.
- Left onto Zeltenreich Road at 10 miles.
- Right onto Musser School Road at 10.5 miles.
- Left onto Groffdale Road at 11.5 miles.
- Right onto East Eby Road at 11.7 miles.
- Left onto Stumptown Road at 12.7 miles.
- Left onto Monterey Road at 14.7 miles.
- Left to Miller's Store at 15.6 miles.
- Return to Monterey Road.
- Right onto Church Road at 15.9 miles.
- Left onto Beechdale Road at 16.8 miles.
- Left onto Old Philadelphia Pike at 17.1 miles.
- Right to finish at 17.2 miles.

such as quilts, chairs, and lamps. Because there's no middleman, the prices are generally rather low.

The first 5 miles of the ride take you through a succession of dairy farms. When you turn onto Harvest Road, you come to a large orchard. You'll see apples on your left and peaches on your right. If they look tempting, you can stop at Kauffman's Market, at the intersection of Old Philadelphia Pike and Harvest Road, to try them. Kauffman's has all sorts of stuff to refresh you, and there's even a picnic table under a tree.

On North Harvest Road is an Amish farm with a sign that says simply QUILTS. The lady of the house uses a manual sewing machine to produce quilts that she sells to customers all over the country.

On Newport Road you will find a one-room school. The Amish educate their children in these schools, and they're still building new ones.

Soon after you turn onto Scenic Road, you'll understand how it got its name. Although you will not have done any serious climbing, you'll have a great view of a little valley dotted with farms and silos. At the intersection of Stumptown and Mascot roads, there's a park on one side of the road. On the other side is the Mascot Roller Mill. Tours are available from May through October.

Natural-food fans will enjoy a visit to Miller's Store on Monterey Road. There's a green sign out front, just before a little stream. This is a well-stocked health-food store operated on an Amish farm. People drive a long way to stock up and save. Prices are considerably lower than in the mall. If you come during harvest months—July through October—you'll find big crates of pears, plums, apples, and other fruits sitting out front.

Blue Ball

Number of miles:	13 or 19.6
Approximate pedaling time:	1 or 1½ hours
Terrain:	Rolling
Surface:	Fair, several rough spots
Things to see:	Farms, town of Churchtown, covered bridge, magnificent old houses
Food:	Shady Maple Market (at start and end)
Facilities:	Shady Maple Market
Options:	6.6-mile extension; connection with New Holland ride

On the roads around Blue Ball, the automobile is not king. In fact, it's probably number three in popularity, behind the horse and buggy and the bicycle. As you ride on these roads, you're likely to find more bikes than you'll see anywhere outside of China. The area has a large Mennonite population. While Mennonites do have cars, they regard them primarily as utilitarian transport vehicles; so they often choose a bike over a car for a reasonably short trip.

This ride doesn't have any attractions that draw thousands of visitors along the way. What it offers is an opportunity to ride with minimal interference from cars. There's probably not a spot on this ride where you can't see at least one farm. If you ride on a summer morning, you'll find entire families working in the fields. Father may be on the tractor while mother and children pick crops, pull weeds, or put plants into the ground.

Early in the ride there is a covered bridge. If you've never ridden through one, be cautious. They're narrow and dark. Don't enter if there's a vehicle coming in the other direction.

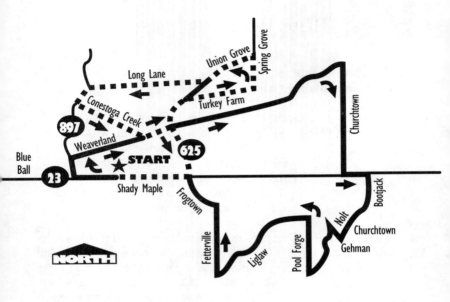

NOTE: ■ ■ ■ INDICATES RIDE EXTENSION

Spring Grove

Union Grove

Long Lane

Churchtown

Conestoga Creek

Turkey Farm

897

Weaverland

625

Blue Ball

23

START

Shady Maple

Frogtown

Bootjack

NORTH

Fetterville

Liglaw

Pool Forge

Nolt

Churchtown

Gehman

HOW to get there Shady Maple Market in Blue Ball, where you start, is on Route 23, between Route 897 and Route 625, just east of Route 23's intersection with U.S. Route 322. Take the Pennsylvania Turnpike to the Morgantown exit. Get off the Turnpike and go west on Route 23.

DIREC-TIONS for the ride

- Leave the Shady Maple parking lot and go west (left) on Route 23.
- Right onto Route 897 at 0.5 mile.
- Right onto Weaverland Road at 0.9 mile.
- Bear left at fork, toward covered bridge, at 3.4 mile.
- Right onto Churchtown Road at 4.1 miles.
- Left onto Route 23 at 5.9 miles.
- Right onto Bootjack Road at 6.3 miles.
- Right onto Windsor Road at 6.5 miles.
- Left onto Churchtown Road at 7.0 miles.
- Right onto Nolt Road at 7.4 miles.
- Left onto Gehman Road at 7.6 miles.
- Right onto Pool Forge Road at 8.6 miles.
- Left onto Liglaw Road at 9.3 miles.
- Right onto Fetterville Road at 11.3 miles.
- Left onto Frogtown Road at 11.9 miles.
- Left onto Route 23 at 12.5 miles to Shady Maple.

To extend the ride 6.6 miles

- After turning onto Route 23 (see direction above) turn right onto Route 625 at 12.7 miles.
- Right onto Turkey Farm Road at 13.8 miles.
- Left onto Spring Grove Road at 14.3 miles.
- Left onto Union Grove Road at 15.1 miles.
- Left onto Route 625 at 15.4 miles.
- Right onto Long Lane at 15.7 miles.
- Left onto Route 897 at 16.5 miles.
- Left onto Conestoga Creek Road at 16.9 miles.
- Left onto Weaverland Road at 18 .0 miles.
- Right onto Route 625 at 18.3 miles.
- Right onto Route 23 at 19.1 miles.
- Finish at Shady Maple at 19.6 miles.

Note: You can easily connect this ride with the New Holland ride (page 91). The place where they join is the intersection of Union Grove Road and Route 625. To pick up the New Holland ride, go straight instead of turning left onto Route 625. This will put you on Fairview Avenue, at the 8.4-mile mark of the New Holland ride.

Churchtown, the main settlement on the ride, is a small village named for its high number of churches. Today it sports antiques and craft shops. It also offers a great view of the valley to the north. On Windsor Road, just outside of Churchtown, stands one of the biggest houses that you'll see anywhere. But mostly you'll see farms.

This is a great place to ride for the sake of riding. And on a pristine autumn afternoon, this is as pretty as a ride can be.

The big day of the year in Blue Ball is Blue Ball Day, the Saturday before Labor Day. It's the town's big celebration. They have a pancake breakfast, a 5-mile run, craft shows, and all sorts of entertainment and food. For at least that one day, the streets of Blue Ball are a busy place.

Ephrata

Number of miles:	16.7
Approximate pedaling time:	1½ hours
Terrain:	Flat
Surface:	Good
Things to see:	Ephrata Cloister, Ephrata Playhouse, Green Dragon Market, Doneckers
Food:	In Ephrata and at Green Dragon
Facilities:	At Ephrata Cloister, park in Ephrata, and Green Dragon

Ephrata (EF-ruh-tuh) is a not-so-small town in the heart of the Pennsylvania Dutch country. The ride begins at the Ephrata Cloister. The Cloister, one of the first communal societies in America, flourished during the eighteenth century. The residents led an austere life, focusing on spiritual rather than materialistic goals. The Cloister also became an early center for printing and publishing. Ten of the original buildings have been restored to recreate the original Cloister.

After you leave the Cloister, you'll ride through Ephrata for several miles. On Vine Street you'll see the Playhouse In The Park. This is a home for summer theater; there's a good selection of plays every year. If you're in town on the Fourth of July, you might want to stop at Ephrata High School, on Oak Street, and do the Firecracker 5-mile run.

At the 1.8-mile mark, you'll have to cross a busy highway. It's much easier if you go to the traffic light at the Diamond SpringWater Company. Once you turn onto Rettew Mill Road, the traffic is over for a while. You'll go through a covered bridge and out into the country, and until you get to the Green Dragon, you'll be riding among farms and occasional orchards.

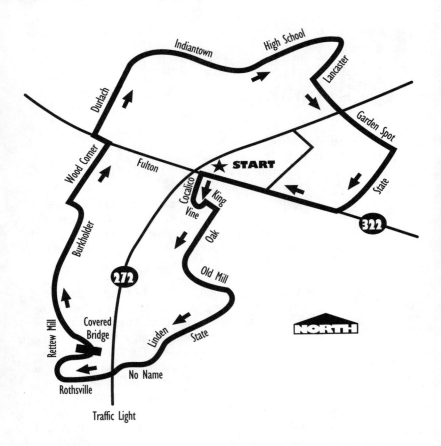

Indiantown

High School

Lancaster

Durlach

Garden Spot

Wood Corner

Fulton

★ **START**

State

Cocalico

King

Vine

Burkholder

Oak

272

Old Mill

Covered
Bridge

NORTH

State

Rettew Mill

Linden

No Name

Rothsville

Traffic Light

322

HOW
to get
there

The Ephrata Cloister is on West Main Street (U.S. Route 322) in Ephrata, right beside Route 272. (Route 322 also intersects U.S. Route 222, just east of town. And Route 222 has an interchange with the Pennsylvania Turnpike about 5 miles north of Ephrata.) Get off the Pennsylvania Turnpike at the Reading/Lancaster interchange and go south on Route 272. You'll see signs for U.S. Route 322 and for the Cloister.

- Leave the Cloister and go right on Main Street (U.S. Route 322).
- Right onto Fulton Street and then onto Cocalico Street, just after you cross a creek, at 0.2 mile.
- Stay on the road beside the creek.
- Left onto Vine Street at 0.5 mile.
- Right onto King Street at 0.6 mile.
- Right onto Oak Street at 0.7 mile.
- Left onto Old Mill Road at 1.0 mile.
- Right onto State Street at 1.5 miles.
- Left onto Linden Avenue at 1.7 miles.
- Right onto unnamed street at 1.8 miles to traffic light.
- Cross highway onto Rothsville Road.
- Right onto Rettew Mill Road at 2.2 miles.
- Straight at 4.1 miles onto Burkholder Road.
- Right onto Wood Corner Road at 4.6 miles.
- Left onto U.S. Route 322 and quickly right onto Durlach Road at 5.5 miles.
- Right onto Indiantown Road at 6.5 miles.
- Left onto High School Road at 10.0 miles.
- Right onto Lancaster Avenue at 11.2 miles.
- Lancaster turns into Line Road.
- Left onto Garden Spot Road at 13.0 miles.
- Cross highway at 13.5 miles; continue on Garden Spot Road.
- Right onto State Street at 14.2 miles.
- Right onto Main Street at 16.0 miles.
- Left into Cloister at 16.7 miles.

The Green Dragon Market—open only on Fridays—is a living demonstration of capitalism at work. The market's brochures state that "If you can't buy it at the Green Dragon, 'it chust ain't fer sale.'" And that's only a slight exaggeration. Certainly, if anybody's ever eaten it, you can find it at the Green Dragon. Fruits and vegetables of every sort are for sale. And because there are fifty other people selling the same items, the prices stay low. There are also restaurants and french fry stands and taco stands and. . . . You'll also find clothes, quilts, toys, books, shoes, chairs, auto supplies, and hundreds of other items for sale. Occasionally there will also be hundreds of trucks loaded with hay; they auction that off too.

After you leave the Dragon, you'll come to Doneckers. This is another place where you can buy food and clothes, but it's slightly different from the Green Dragon. You might even call it exclusive. People come great distances to shop for ladies' apparel sold here. And they have a restaurant that specializes in French cuisine—a far cry from the Dragon. On Main Street you'll find all sorts of stores and restaurants (in case you can't make it on a Friday).

Intercourse

Number of miles:	16.2
Approximate pedaling time:	1½ hours
Terrain:	Rolling
Surface:	Fair; be wary of ruts worn by horses
Things to see:	People's Place, Amish farms, covered bridge
Food:	Many places to eat in Intercourse; roadside produce stands
Facilities:	At Paradise Park

This is a ride through lush Amish farmlands, over lightly traveled roads.

The little town of Intercourse is a curious melting pot. On Main Street you'll see Amish farmers buying supplies while visitors from all over the world buy souvenirs. You'll find horses and buggies tied up beside Cadillacs.

The primary tourist attraction in Intercourse is The People's Place, a group of shops featuring local Amish and Mennonite crafts. There's also a slide show that explains Amish life. Bikers passing through town often stop at Zimmerman's General Store for cold drinks.

You may encounter a little traffic on Route 340, but as soon as you turn onto West View Road, the serious traffic will end. Then it's farm after farm after farm. Keep your eyes open, though, and you'll notice signs advertising interesting items such as metal products, quilts, and even gravity boxes (old-fashioned manure spreaders). You'll also be likely to see farmers using teams of horses and mules to pull their plows, and you'll probably meet some horses and buggies. Keep in mind that a bicycle is generally faster than a buggy.

Spring Garden Road gives you a great downhill run. It's not espe-

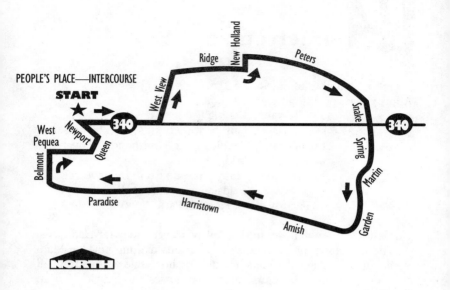

PEOPLE'S PLACE—INTERCOURSE
START

West View · Ridge · New Holland · Peters

Newport · Queen · 340 · Snake

West Pequea · Belmont · Spring · 340

Paradise · Harristown · Amish · Martin · Garden

NORTH

HOW to get there Intercourse lies at the intersection of Pennsylvania Routes 340 and 772, about 10 miles east of Lancaster. Route 340 runs north of and parallel to U.S. Route 30. Route 772 begins on Route 30, near Gap. The People's Place, where the ride begins, is right on 340.

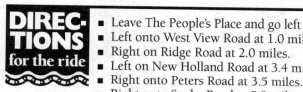

DIRECTIONS for the ride

- Leave The People's Place and go left on Route 340.
- Left onto West View Road at 1.0 mile.
- Right on Ridge Road at 2.0 miles.
- Left on New Holland Road at 3.4 miles.
- Right onto Peters Road at 3.5 miles.
- Right onto Snake Road at 5.9 miles.
- Merge into Spring Garden Road and cross Route 340 at 7.1 miles.
- Right onto Martin Road, and
- Left onto Spring Garden Road at 7.6 miles.
- Right onto Amish Road at 8.7 miles.
- Right onto Harristown Road at 10.7 miles.
- Right onto Belmont Road at 13.2 miles.
- Right onto West Pequea (peck way) Lane at 15.0 miles.
- Left onto Queen Road at 15.5 miles.
- Left onto Newport Road at 16.0 miles.
- Merge left into Old Philadelphia Pike (Route 340) to finish at 16.2 miles.

cially steep, but you should be able to hit 30 MPH without any effort. When you reach the intersection of Harristown and Belmont roads, you're in Paradise. To your left will be U.S. Route 30. After you turn onto Belmont, you'll see a covered bridge. Before you reach it, however, you'll see Londonvale Road on your left. If you're looking for a place to stop and relax, there's a nice park about half a mile down Londonvale Road.

Be careful going through the covered bridge. The boards go in the same direction as you're traveling, and it's possible to catch a tire and take a spill. If you're uncomfortable, it's best to walk the bike through. In case you're wondering, covered bridges got their covers to protect the wooden planks from the weather.

On Queen Lane is a woodworking shop that makes some very impressive weathervanes. At the end of the ride, be careful as you get back onto Route 340. It's a tricky intersection.

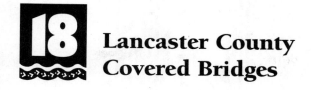

Lancaster County Covered Bridges

Number of miles:	33.3
Approximate pedaling time:	3¹⁄₂ hours
Terrain:	Mostly rolling, several tough climbs
Surface:	Fair
Things to see:	Five covered bridges, America's oldest pretzel bakery, polo matches
Food:	Many places on route
Facilities:	In Lititz, Rothsville, Brownstown

Lancaster County leads the nation in the covered-bridge category, with twenty-four bridges still in use. This ride takes you through five of them, and on a tour of scenic farmlands.

The ride begins in Lititz, a tree-lined town that is home to the Sturgis Pretzel Bakery, the self-proclaimed first pretzel bakery in America. Established in 1861, the bakery allows visitors to watch pretzels being made and to twist their own. Lititz also features It's Only Natural, a natural foods store/macrobiotic restaurant on East Front Street, and the Wilbur Chocolate Company on North Broad Street, right beside Lititz Springs Park.

Just before you come to the first covered bridge, you'll see Hoover's Farm Market, an excellent source of farm-fresh produce. On Church Street in Rothsville is the Lancaster Polo Club. Matches take place on Sunday afternoons from May through September. Malcolm Forbes used to ride his motorcycle to Lancaster County to dine at the Brownstown Restaurant, at 10.6 miles.

At 14.7 miles you'll see a road sign that reads PASHING WEEG. Underneath is the English translation—PEACH ROAD. *Pashing weeg* is Pennsylvania Dutch, a German dialect spoken only in a small part of

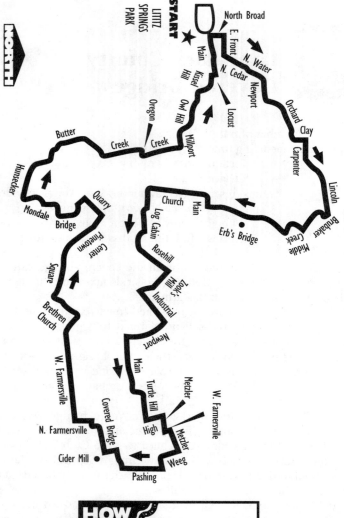

NORTH

START
LITITZ SPRINGS PARK

North Broad
E. Front
N. Water
Main
Kissel Hill
N. Cedar
Newport
Locust
Orchard
Clay
Oregon
Owl Hill
Millport
Carpenter
Butter
Creek
Creek
Lincoln
Brubaker Creek
Middle Creek
Hunsecker
Church
Main
Log Cabin
Quarry
Erb's Bridge
Mondale
Bridge
Rosehill
Pinetown
Center
Zook's Mill
Square
Industrial
Newport
Brethren Church
Main
W. Farmersville
Metzler
W. Farmersville
Covered Bridge
Turtle Hill
N. Farmersville
High
Metzler
Cider Mill
Weeg
Pashing

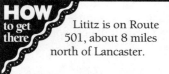

HOW to get there

Lititz is on Route 501, about 8 miles north of Lancaster.

- Begin at Lititz Springs Park, on Route 501 in Lititz, beside the railroad tracks.
- Left (north) onto North Broad Street.
- Right onto E. Front Street at 0.1 mile.
- Left onto N. Cedar Street at 0.3 mile.
- Left onto N. Water Street at 0.8 mile.
- Right onto Newport Road at 1.0 mile.
- Left onto Orchard Road at 1.3 miles.
- Left onto Clay Road at 2.5 miles.
- Right onto Carpenter Road at 2.8 miles.
- Straight onto Lincoln Road at 3.4 miles.
- Right onto Brubaker Road at 4.1 miles.
- Left onto Brubaker Road at 4.2 miles.
- Right onto Middle Creek Road at 4.9 miles.
- Right onto Erb's Bridge Road at 5.1 miles.
- Covered Bridge at 5.5 miles.
- Right onto Main Street (Rothsville) at 6.8 miles.
- Left onto Church Street at 6.8 miles.
- Left onto Log Cabin Road at 8.0 miles.
- Covered Bridge at 9.0 miles.
- Left onto Rosehill Road at 9.0 miles.
- Right onto Zook's Mill Road at 9.4 miles.
- Left onto Industrial Road at 9.9 miles.
- Right onto Newport Road at 10.2 miles.
- Left onto Main Street (Brownstown) at 10.6 miles.
- Right onto Turtle Hill Road at 11.9 miles.
- Left onto High Road at 12.6 miles.
- Right onto Metzler Road at 13.1 miles.
- Left onto W. Farmersville Road at 13.5 miles.
- Right onto Metzler Road at 13.6 miles.
- Right onto Pashing Weeg at 14.7 miles.
- Right onto Cider Mill Road at 15.3 miles.
- Covered Bridge at 15.7 miles.
- Right onto Covered Bridge at 15.8 miles.
- Left onto N. Farmersville Road at 17.0 miles.

- Right onto W. Farmersville Road at 17.4 miles.
- Left onto Brethren Church Road at 18.3 miles.
- Right onto Center Square Road at 19.1 miles.
- Right onto Quarry Road at 22.0 miles.
- Left onto Pinetown Road at 23.2 miles.
- Left onto Bridge Road at 23.7 miles.
- Covered Bridge at 23.7 miles.
- Right onto Mondale Road at 24.3 miles.
- Right onto Hunsecker Road at 25.4 miles.
- Right onto Butter Road at 26.3 miles.
- Butter Road becomes Creek Road.
- Cross Route 272 at 27.6 miles.
- Right onto Oregon Road at 28 miles.
- Immediate left onto Creek Road at 28 miles.
- Left onto Millport Road at 29.6 miles.
- Right onto Owl Hill Road at 29.7 miles.
- Right onto Kissel Hill Road at 31.8 miles.
- Right onto Locust Street at 32.4 miles.
- Left onto Main Street at 32.7 miles.
- Right onto N. Broad Street at 33.2 miles and finish at 33.3 miles.

Pennsylvania. it combines elements of English and German, and many of its speakers are Amish and Mennonite.

The third covered bridge presents the best chance to see a scene from 100 years ago—a horse and buggy going through a covered bridge. Many Amish and Mennonite families live right around this bridge, and they travel primarily by buggy. At 17.4 miles you'll come to the four-way street, intersection of North/South Farmersville Road and East/West Farmersville Road.

The final two covered bridges on the ride took a beating from Hurricane Agnes in 1972. The Pinetown Bridge floated several miles downstream, but it remained intact, and workers managed to replace it. The raging waters destroyed the original Hunsecker Bridge, and a new one went up in 1975.

Middle Creek

Number of miles:	16.4
Approximate pedaling time:	1½ hours
Terrain:	Rolling, with many flat sections
Surface:	Good
Things to see:	Middle Creek Wildlife Management Area, fertile farms
Food:	In Richland, halfway through ride
Facilities:	At Visitor Center at start of ride and at park in Richland

This ride is definitely for bird lovers. Middle Creek Wildlife Management Area is a 5,000-acre preserve dedicated to the propagation and protection of wildlife, particularly geese and ducks. The most common species is the Canada goose. Thousands stop here to feed, and some make this their permanent home. The birds are most plentiful during their migratory flights in spring and fall. The preserve also has walking trails, picnic areas, and a Visitor Center. You might want to combine this bike ride with a hike. Outside the preserve, the farmlands and small towns of Lebanon County provide a nice place to ride with little traffic.

As you ride down Hopeland Road at the very beginning of the ride, you'll pass a big lake. Here you can see hundreds or thousands of birds—and probably some bird watchers with binoculars. In addition to the geese, you may see bluebirds, swallows, redwings, and many more species. Even eagles have made occasional appearances. In the wooded areas there are many deer, and there have been several sightings of wild turkeys. But if you're unfamiliar with wildlife, don't worry; nothing around here will do you any harm.

At the end of Hopeland Road, you'll come to the tiny town of Kle-

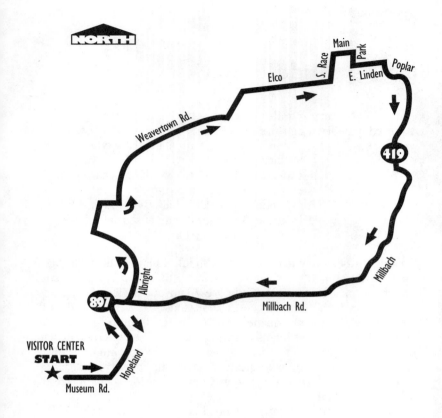

NORTH

Main
S. Race
Elco
Park
E. Linden
Poplar

Weavertown Rd.

419

Millbach

Albright

897

Millbach Rd.

VISITOR CENTER
START

Hopeland

Museum Rd.

HOW
to get
there
Middle Creek Wildlife Management Area lies on Route 897, south of Lebanon. It can also be reached by U.S. Route 322. Take 322 west from Ephrata or east from Route 501 to Clay. Turn north on Clay Road and follow the signs to Middle Creek.

DIREC-TIONS
for the ride

- Leave the Middle Creek Visitor Center on Museum Road and go left on Hopeland Road, the main road through the preserve .
- Right onto Route 897 south at 2.5 miles.
- Left onto Albright Road at 2.6 miles.
- Bend to left at intersection with Chapel Road.
- Right on Route 419 (no sign) at T intersection at 4.8 miles.
- Left onto Weavertown Road (no sign) at 5.1 miles.
- Bear right on Weavertown at 5.9 miles.
- Right onto Elco Drive at 7.1 miles.
- Left onto South Race Avenue in Richland at 8.6 miles.
- Right onto Main Street (before tracks) at 8.9 miles.
- Right onto Park Street at 9.1 miles.
- Left onto East Linden Avenue at 9.4 miles.
- Right onto Poplar Street (toward Millbach) at 9.6 miles.
- Bend to left at 9.8 miles.
- Left onto Route 419 at T intersection at 11.3 miles.
- Right onto Millbach Road at 11.4 miles.
- Right onto Route 897 north at 14.0 miles.
- Left onto Hopeland Road at 14.1 miles.
- Right onto Museum Road at 16.4 miles.

infeltersville; then you'll move into farming territory. This is some of the most productive agricultural land in the world. If you come at the right time of year, you'll see fields bursting with corn, beans, melons, and much more. It wouldn't be a bad idea to bring a spoon, just in case you happen upon a good cantaloupe at one of the roadside stands.

About halfway through the ride, you'll come into Richland, a little town with a Norman Rockwell look to it. Here, you can get a brief glimpse of small town life. You can park your bike and walk from one end of the business district to the other in a couple of minutes. You'll find food and cold drinks here.

After you pass through Richland, it's back into the country and more pleasant riding. You may even see a horse and buggy on the roads.

ICE HOUSE

THIS MASSIVE EXCAVATION WAS FILLED
WITH ICE BLOCKS CUT FROM THE ESTATE POND.
INSULATED WITH SAWDUST, IT
SUPPLIED ICE TO THE MANSION FOR ONE
FULL YEAR. SUSPENDED INSIDE ARE THE
ORIGINAL POLES USED TO RETRIEVE THE ICE.

Mount Gretna/ Mount Hope

Number of miles:	14.6
Approximate pedaling time:	1½ hours
Terrain:	Flat to rolling with one steep hill
Surface:	Good
Things to see:	Mount Hope Winery, Renaissance Faire, Mount Gretna Playhouse, lake in Mount Gretna, Governor Dick Tower, Hampshire Orchards, Frey's Herb Farm
Food:	Store, bakery, and ice cream shop in Mount Gretna; apples and other fruit at Hampshire Orchards
Facilities:	At Mount Hope and in Mount Gretna
Option:	Connection with Speedwell Forge ride

Here's a short ride with a lot of interesting sights along the way. Mount Hope, the former mansion of a wealthy early American iron-mine owner, is now a winery, and the grounds are a vineyard. Many different events take place on the grounds. On weekends from July through September, the Pennsylvania Renaissance Faire re-creates the splendor of sixteenth-century England. Hundreds of colorfully attired performers joust, juggle, and jest. There are also a Fifties Revival and a Dickens Christmas, in addition to wine making.

On Camp Road you'll see Hampshire Orchards. This is an unusual orchard in that it's basically new. Its thousands of neatly planted young trees were just coming into full production in 1989. Here you can get apples and peaches directly from the trees, as well as freshly made cider and other apple products. Just down the road is Frey's Herb Farm, a good place to stock up on parsley, sage, thyme, and so on.

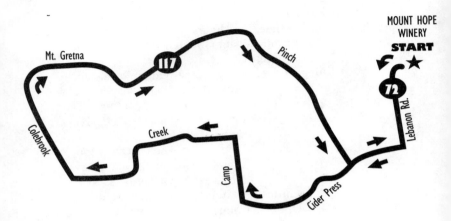

MOUNT HOPE
WINERY
START ★

Mt. Gretna

117

Pinch

Colebrook

Creek

Camp

Cider Press

Lebanon Rd.

72

HOW
to get
there

Take the Pennsylvania Turnpike to the Lancaster/Lebanon exit. Exit onto Route 72 and go south, toward Lancaster. Mount Hope Estate is right beside the turnpike, on Route 72, north of Lancaster and south of Lebanon.

DIREC-TIONS for the ride

- Leave the parking lot at Mount Hope and go left (south) on Route 72 (Lebanon Road).
- Right on Cider Press Road at 0.5 mile.
- Right onto Camp Road at 3.2 miles.
- Left onto Creek Road at 3.7 miles.
- Right onto Colebrook Road at 5.4 miles.
- Right onto Mount Gretna Road (Route 117) at 7.9 miles.
- Right onto Pinch Road at 10.8 miles.
- Left onto Cider Press Road at 13.6 miles.
- Left onto Route 72 (Lebanon Road) at 14.1 miles.
- Right into Mount Hope at 14.6 miles.

Note: You can easily connect this ride with the Speedwell Forge ride (page 101). To do so, when you hit Route 72 (Lebanon Road) at the 14.1-mile mark, go straight onto Mountain Road instead of turning left. Three miles down Mountain Road, you'll come to Sanctuary Road, which is the 5.2-mile mark of the Speedwell Forge ride.

For a while the ride rolls through farms and a golf course. On Colebrook Road you'll climb a little, cross over the Pennsylvania Turnpike, and move into a section of State Game Lands. The farms will end, and the woods will begin.

Mount Gretna is an appealing little town with something to interest almost everyone. The lake, open for public swimming, is inviting on a hot day. It must also be inviting on New Year's Day, because several hundred "Polar Bears" dive in every year, even when they have to break the ice to do so. During the summer, Mount Gretna is a vacation home for some families. Its main attractions are its quiet and events such as art shows. There's also a playhouse with a full summer schedule and an equally busy concert series. For refreshments, there are an ice cream shop and a general store. There's also an antiques shop. If you were to wake up and find yourself in Mount Gretna, you'd probably think that you were somewhere in New England.

Although you can't see many of them from the main road, there are some magnificent houses in Gretna, tucked away among the evergreen trees that cover most of the area. To see them, go up any of the side streets to your right.

You'll hit the ride's one good hill as you leave Gretna on Pinch Road. But it's not all bad. At the top of the hill is a big stone slab with a marker commemorating Governor Dick, and if you follow the trail, you come to a big tower that you can climb for a great view of the surrounding valleys.

New Holland

Number of miles:	47 or 15.1
Approximate pedaling time:	4½ hours/1½ hours
Terrain:	Some of everything—flat stretches to good hills
Surface:	Fair
Things to see:	Pennsylvania Dutch country, Amish farms, antiques shops, small towns, zoo
Food:	In New Holland, Terre Hill, Bowmansville, Adamstown, and Martindale
Facilities:	At parks in New Holland, Terre Hill, Adamstown, and Bowmansville
Options:	Detour back to start for shorter ride; connection with Blue Ball ride

This is a longer ride that will take you through the farmlands of eastern Lancaster County. (For less ambitious riders, there's an optional shorter ride of 15.1 miles.) Many of these farms are owned and operated by the "Plain People," Amish and Mennonites. Members of these religious sects avoid modern conveniences such as cars or electricity.

The terrain makes this a fairly difficult ride. Around Adamstown and Bowmansville, it's quite hilly. But there are no hills that a strong rider can't handle.

New Holland is the first and the last town on the ride. This is a busy place where Plain People mix with their "English" neighbors. The biggest industry in town is the Ford New Holland plant, where they produce the most modern of farm equipment. Ironically, the plant sits right beside Amish farms that still use horses to pull the plows. At the New Holland Community Park, where the ride begins,

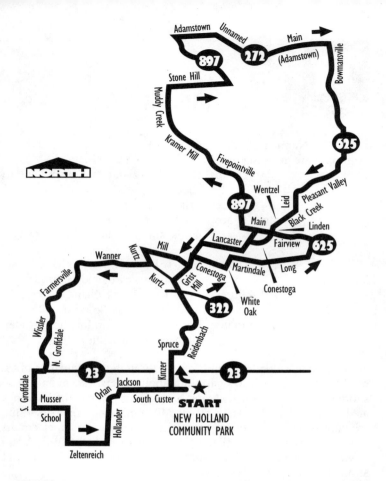

HOW to get there New Holland is on Pennsylvania Route 23, about 10 miles northeast of Lancaster. Route 23 intersects U.S. Route 30 in Lancaster and U.S. 322 in Blue Ball. Take the Pennsylvania Turnpike at Morgantown exit and go west on Route 23. At the Kinzer Avenue traffic light in New Holland, go south (left) on Kinzer Avenue. The New Holland Community Park, where the ride starts, is one block south of Route 23, on Jackson Street.

DIRECTIONS for the ride

- From New Holland Community Park parking area, go left on Jackson Street.
- Right onto Kinzer Avenue at 0.1 mile.
- Right onto Spruce Avenue at 0.8 mile.
- Left onto Reidenbach Road at 0.9 mile.
- Reidenbach Road bends right at 1.5 miles.
- Cross U.S. 322 onto Kurtz Road, at 3.0 miles.

Note: At this point you can opt to take a shorter ride (15.1 miles) by first following these two directions:

- Left onto Wanner Road at 3.8 miles.
- Cross U.S. 322 at 4.7 miles.

Then skip the next thirty-five directions. Pick the directions up again at "Merge straight onto Farmersville Road." (For the rest of the directions, mileage for the shorter option is given in parentheses.)

- Right onto Gristmill Road at 3.4 miles.
- Right onto Conestoga Road at 4.4 miles.
- Left onto White Oak Road at 5.2 miles.
- Right onto Martindale Road at 5.5 miles.
- Left onto Long Lane at 6.0 miles.
- Left onto Route 625 at 8.0 miles.
- Left onto Fairview Avenue (at Terre Hill Mennonite School) at 8.4 miles.
- Fairview becomes Main Street.
- Left onto Conestoga Avenue at 9.8 miles.
- Go through park and right onto Lancaster Avenue.
- Left onto Main Street.
- Right onto Route 897.
- Left onto Fivepointville Road at 12.2 miles.
- Right onto Kramer Mill Road at 12.9 miles.
- Right onto Muddy Creek Road at 14.7 miles.
- Right onto Stone Hill Road at 15.9 miles.
- Left at T intersection (Route 897) at 17.2 miles.

- Right onto Adamstown Road at 20.0 miles.
- Right onto unnamed road at 20.7 miles (white buildings to your right).
- Left on Route 272 at 21.0 miles.
- Bear Left at swimming pool at 21.3 miles.
- Right onto Bowmansville Road at 22.6 miles.
- Right onto Route 625 south at 26.3 miles. (For park in Bowmansville, turn left on Church Road.)
- Right onto Pleasant Valley Road at 27.7 miles.
- Left onto Leid Road at 29.0 miles.
- Right onto Black Creek Road at 29.8 miles.
- Right onto Wentzel Road at 30.8 miles.
- Left onto Linden Avenue at 31.3 miles.
- Right onto Main Street at 31.6 miles.
- Left onto Conestoga Avenue (through park again) at 32.0 miles.
- Left onto Lancaster Avenue.
- Left onto Gristmill Road at 34.3 miles.
- Right onto Mill Road at 34.5 miles.
- Left onto Kurtz Road at 35.3 miles.
- Right onto Wanner Road at 35.6 miles.
- Merge straight onto Farmersville Road at 36.8 miles.
- Farmersville Road bends right at 37.2 miles.
- Left onto Wissler Road at 37.6 miles.
- Merge straight onto North Groffdale Road at 39.6 (7.8) miles.
- Right onto Route 23 at 40.9 (9.1) miles.
- Left onto South Groffdale Road at 41.0 (9.2) miles.
- Left onto Musser School Road at 41.8 (10.0) miles.
- Left onto Zeltenreich Road at 42.9 (11.1) miles.
- Left onto Hollander Road at 43.9 (12.1) miles.
- Right onto Orlan Road at 45.0 (13.2) miles.
- Left onto South Custer Avenue at 45.7 (14.0) miles.
- Right onto West Jackson at 46.0 (14.2) miles.
- Finish at 47.0 (15.1) miles.

Note: You can connect this ride with the Blue Ball ride (page 67). They join at the intersection of Route 625 and Union Grove Road. To pick up the Blue Ball ride, go right on Union Grove Road instead of going left on Fairview Avenue at 8.4 miles. This will put you at the 15.1 mile mark of the Blue Ball ride.

---

there's a full summer schedule of events such as concerts. In early October the New Holland Fair takes over the town. Ferris wheels, food, and agricultural exhibits fill the streets.

You'll leave New Holland and pass through flat farm country for a few miles. The next community is Terre Hill. This is a quiet little place with several restaurants, some beautiful old homes, and a nice little park.

After passing through Terre Hill, you'll be out in farming country for about 10 miles. The next major settlement will be Adamstown. In August Adamstown is home to the Gemutlichkeit (Gumooutlh-kite), sometimes called the Bavarian Beer Festival. On Sundays throughout the year, Adamstown is a major antiques center. Vendors seem to set up almost anywhere.

Down the road from Adamstown is Bowmansville, known to locals as the home of the Ox Trot, a particularly hilly 5-mile running race held on the second Saturday in August. In Bowmansville there are a general store, a park, and a youth hostel.

From Bowmansville you'll go back through Terre Hill and then back to New Holland, but mostly on different roads. All along the way you can expect to see a lot of bicycles. Among the people in this area, the bike is a primary means of transportation. And they don't ride sleek twelve-speeds; three-speeds are much more common. On a Sunday morning you'll see hundreds of young people riding bikes to and from church. Any day of the week, if you hit a traffic jam, it will be more likely to involve buggies and bikes than cars. Many of the cars that you do see will be black. Some will even have black bumpers. Mennonites paint their cars this way as a religious statement.

As you ride, you'll pass many farms. Most will have a stand where they sell their produce and baked goods. Many will also sell such local specialties as shoo-fly pie and homemade root beer.

Quarryville

Number of miles:	21
Approximate pedaling time:	2 hours
Terrain:	Rolling, several good hills
Surface:	Good
Things to see:	Amish farms, scenic vistas, covered bridge
Food:	In Quarryville and Bartville
Facilities:	At start of ride and in Bartville

Quarryville is the only significant town in southern Lancaster County, and the surrounding area offers some great bicycling. Amish families live on many of the farms, and because they travel in buggies, traffic is generally quite light. Quarryville took its name from the many quarries in the area. The limestone that makes the soil rich also makes good stone for building.

Tourists have discovered the other Amish areas of Lancaster County, but the southern end is far off the paths of most visitors. From June until October the predominent feature of the landscape is corn. It covers thousands of acres, and at times it's all that you can see as you ride along. In good years it towers above even the tallest people.

The covered bridge on this ride offers some interesting pictures in hot weather, when cows and horses gather under it to get out of the sun. The Bartville Store, at 7.2 miles, is your only source of supplies on the ride. It's a fairly unusual store in that it has both gas pumps and places for the Amish to tie their horses.

Robert Fulton Highway takes its name from the inventor of the steamboat. His birthplace is about 5 miles south of Quarryville on the highway.

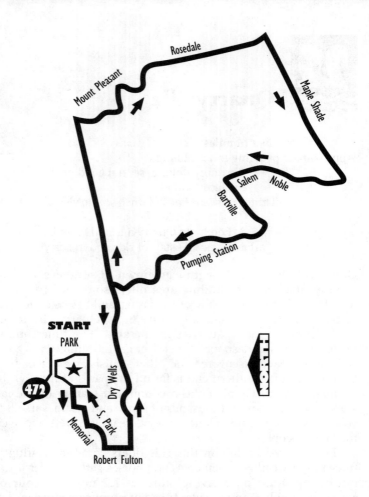

Rosedale

Mount Pleasant

Maple Shade

Salem   Noble

Barryville

Pumping Station

START

PARK

★

472

Dry Wells

S. Park

Memorial

Robert Fulton

NORTH

HOW to get there Quarryville is about 12 miles south of Lancaster, in southern Lancaster County, at the intersection of U.S. 222, Route 372, and Route 472.

DIREC-TIONS
for the ride

- Start at Quarryville Park, Route 472, on the south side of town. Begin at the Hoffman Community Building. Go west toward the swimming pool.
- Left onto Memorial Drive at 0.1 mile.
- Left onto Park Avenue at 0.2 mile.
- Left onto Robert Fulton Highway at 0.8 mile (caution, busy road).
- Left onto Dry Wells Road at 0.9 mile.
- Right onto Mount Pleasant Road at 5.4 miles.
- Left after covered bridge at 6.1 miles.
- Bear right, uphill, at 6.6 miles.
- Straight ahead on Rosedale Road at 7.2 miles (Bartville Store).
- Right onto Maple Shade Road at 9.2 miles.
- Right onto Noble Road at 11.9 miles.
- Left onto Salem Road at 13.6 miles.
- Left onto Bartville Road at 14.2 miles.
- Right onto Pumping Station Road at 15.1 miles.
- Left onto Dry Wells Road at 17.4 miles.
- Right onto Robert Fulton Highway at 20.1 miles.
- Right onto South Park Avenue at 20.2 miles.
- Right onto Memorial Drive at 20.8 miles.
- Finish at 21.0 miles.

Speedwell Forge

Number of miles:	25
Approximate pedaling time:	1¾ hours
Terrain:	Rolling hills
Surface:	Good
Things to see:	Farms and woods
Food:	Produce stand on Fairview Road, at 17.5 miles
Facilities:	At Speedwell Forge Lake and one-room school on Lexington Road
Option:	Connection with Mount Gretna/Mount Hope ride

This ride is the course that's used for the Lancaster YMCA Triathlon. It's very scenic, surely one of the prettiest rides in all the triathlon world, and slightly hilly. And because it's laid out to be a race course, you can cover it without having to make a lot of stops. It's 25 fast miles. If you're interested in seeing how fast you can do it, and in comparing yourself to the triathletes, keep in mind that the best riders do this course in about an hour. But they do have the advantage of having traffic stopped at all the intersections.

As you begin the ride, you pass the upper end of Speedwell Forge Lake. You may see some ducks and geese along here. A little farther down the road, just past Long Lane, is a farm where they raise horses and even have a small arena for showing horses. One of the residents of this farm is a peacock. He likes to strut his stuff by the side of the road.

At 2.3 miles you'll turn onto Mountain Road. Don't let the name alarm you; the road has a hill but nothing resembling a mountain. And it also has a great view of the Pennsylvania Turnpike. You can

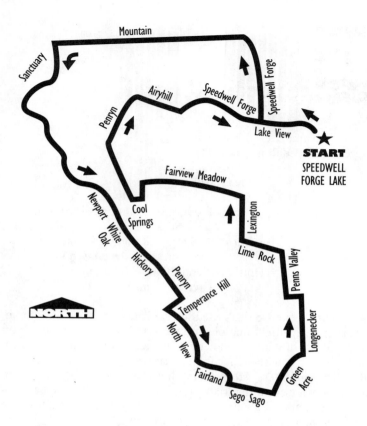

Mountain

Sanctuary

Speedwell Forge

Airyhill

Speedwell Forge

Penryn

Lake View

★
START
SPEEDWELL
FORGE LAKE

Fairview Meadow

Lexington

Newport

White

Oak

Cool
Springs

Hickory

Penryn

Lime Rock

Penns Valley

Temperance Hill

North View

Longenecker

NORTH

Fairland

Sego Sago

Green
Acre

HOW
to get
there
Speedwell Forge Lake is just west of Route 501, north of Lititz and south of Route 501's intersection with U.S. 322. There are signs to it; the ride begins at the lake parking area. You can also reach the lake by getting off the Pennsylvania Turnpike at the Lancaster/Lebanon interchange and going south to Route 72. Then go right on Mountain Road, right on Speedwell Forge Road, and left on Lake View Road to the parking area.

DIRECTIONS for the ride

Note: While you're riding this route, you'll see arrows and mile markers painted on the road. If you wish to follow them, look for mile markers that say LONG BIKE.

- From the parking area at Speedwell Forge Lake, go north, the only possible way, on Lake View Road.
- Merge right onto Speedwell Forge Road at 1.0 mile.
- Left onto Mountain Road at 2.3 miles.
- Left onto Sanctuary Road at 5.2 miles.
- Bear right, staying on Sanctuary, at 5.9 miles.
- Bear left, staying on Sanctuary, at 6.2 miles.
- Left onto Newport Road at 6.5 miles.
- Straight onto White Oak Road at 6.8 miles.
- Left onto Hickory Road at 8.3 miles.
- Right onto Penryn Road at 8.9 miles.
- Right onto Temperance Hill Road at 10.9 miles.
- Left onto North View Road at 11.1 miles.
- Left on Fairland Road at 12.0 miles.
- Left onto Sego Sago Road at 12.7 miles.
- Left onto Green Acres Road at 13.4 miles.
- Left onto Longenecker Road at 13.9 miles.
- Left onto Temperance Hill Road at 14.7 miles.
- Right onto Penns Valley Road at 14.8 miles.
- Left onto Lime Rock Road at 15.0 miles.
- Bear right, across railroad tracks, onto Lexington Road at 15.5 miles.
- Left and right, staying on Lexington, at 16.8 miles.
- Left onto Fairview Road at 17.5 miles.
- Left onto Meadow Road at 19.5 miles.
- Right onto Cool Springs Road at 20.0 miles.
- Right onto Penryn Road at 20.3 miles.
- Right onto Airy Hill Road at 22.8 miles.
- Left onto Speedwell Forge Road at 23.5 miles.
- Sharp right onto Lake View Road at 24.6 miles.
- Finish at 25.6 miles.

Note: This ride connects easily to the Mount Gretna/Mount Hope Ride (page 87). To make the connection, at the 5.2 mile mark, instead of turning left on Sanctuary Road, go straight on Mountain Road. This will take you to Route 72. When you reach 72, you can turn right and go half a mile to the Mount Hope Estate and the beginning of the Mount Gretna/Mount Hope ride, or you can cross 72 onto Cider Press Road and pick up the ride there.

---

look with compassion on the people trapped in their gasoline monsters.

There aren't any tourist attractions on this ride. You'll just ramble along on country roads amidst corn fields, soybean fields (they're the hairy little pods), cows, and sheep. It's not unusual to ride for three or five minutes without seeing a car.

On Lexington Road you'll see a little green one-room schoolhouse. There are outhouses behind the school if you really need them. On Fairview Road is a fruit stand where they sell the fruits and vegetables from the adjacent farm.

After that it's more country roads to the finish. Be careful on Speedwell Forge Road at the end of the ride. You go down a steep hill and have to make a very sharp right. Don't try to take the turn at high speed.

Strasburg

Number of miles:	14.5
Approximate pedaling time:	1½ hours
Terrain:	Rolling
Surface:	Fair
Things to see:	Strasburg RailRoad, Railroad Museum of Pennsylvania, Toy Train Museum, Amish farms, verdant valley
Food:	At beginning of ride and in Strasburg
Facilities:	At beginning and end of ride; none on course

This is a ride on which it seems that there's always something interesting to see. There are tourist attractions and beautiful scenery. And there are country roads with very little traffic.

The Strasburg RailRoad, the starting point for the ride, is the first point of interest. This is America's oldest short-line railroad. The train ride it offers won't really take you anywhere, but it's a nice way to see the farm country between Strasburg and Paradise. The trains are open-air cars pulled by old coal-burning engines. Adjacent to the Strasburg RailRoad is the RailRoad Museum of Pennsylvania, with a large collection of trains and related items. If you're a real train lover, you can spend a night at the Red Caboose Motel; all the rooms are actual cabooses.

As you head out on the ride, you'll be able to keep pace with the trains, and you'll cross the tracks several times. If you carry your camera, you can get some nice pictures. The rail line goes through one of the prettiest farm areas anywhere. The small farms form a patchwork quilt of brown earth and green crops. As you ride east

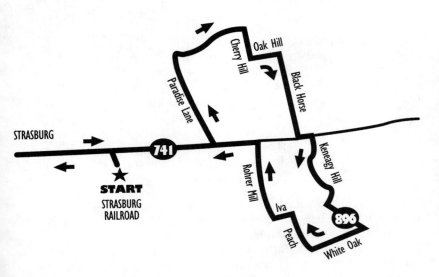

STRASBURG

741

★
START
STRASBURG
RAILROAD

Oak Hill

Cherry Hill

Black Horse

Paradise Lane

Keneagy Hill

Rohrer Mill

Iva

896

Peach

White Oak

HOW
to get
there
Strasburg is at the intersection of Routes 741 and 896, about 10 miles southeast of Lancaster. Route 896 intersects U.S. Route 30; Route 741 intersects U.S. 222 and Route 41. To reach the start of the ride at the Strasburg RailRoad, take Route 741 east out of Strasburg center.

**DIREC-
TIONS**
for the ride

- From the Strasburg RailRoad, head east on Route 741.
- Left on Paradise Lane at 0.5 mile.
- Paradise Lane turns right at 1.8 miles.
- Right onto Cherry Hill Lane at 3.1 miles.
- Left onto Oak Hill Road at 3.8 miles.
- Right onto Black Horse Road at 4.2 miles.
- Left onto Route 741 at 5.7 miles.
- Right onto Keneagy Hill Road at 5.7 miles.
- Left onto Route 896 at T intersection at 7.4 miles.
- Right onto White Oak Road at 8.1 miles.
- Right onto Peach Road at 8.5 miles.
- Left onto Iva Road (sharp turn at bottom of hill) at 9.5 miles.
- Right onto Rohrer Mill Road at 9.9 miles.
- Cross Route 896 at 10.3 miles.
- Left onto Route 741 (Strasburg Road) at 11.3 miles.
- Straight to traffic light in Strasburg 13.5 miles.
- Turn around and return to Strasburg RailRoad 14.5 miles.

from Strasburg, you'll notice that green is the dominant color. The valley is incredibly lush and verdant.

Many of the farms belong to Amish families and are meticulously neat and exceptionally productive. On the roads you're bound to come up behind a horse and buggy somewhere, and you'll find produce being sold directly from the farms. There is no sweeter sweet corn anywhere.

The ride includes one good hill, on Keneagy Hill Road. But the view from the top makes the little climb worthwhile.

The end of the ride brings you into the small, historic town of Strasburg. Many of the buildings sport plaques that indicate their historic importance. In town you'll find many places to eat and a variety of shops. There are a general store, a baseball card shop, and antiques shops. Strasburg is a good place to find Amish arts and crafts and to relax after your ride.

Biglerville

Number of miles:	17
Approximate pedaling time:	1¾ hours
Terrain:	Mostly flat, some rolling hills
Surface:	Good
Things to see:	Apple orchards, Penn State Fruit Research Farm, Apple Blossom Festival, Apple Harvest Festival
Food:	Kennie's Market and restaurants in Biglerville; General Store in Arendtsville
Facilities:	At Oak Park (15.5 miles)

The best time to take this ride is late April and early May when the fruit trees blossom. At several points on the ride, apple, peach, pear, and cherry trees will be all that you can see. Adams County is the heart of Pennsylvania's fruit-growing region, and Biglerville is the center for the production of apple products. Several big companies, such as Musselman's, have plants here. Pedaling through this quiet, scenic area can be a delight.

The ride begins in downtown Biglerville, a metropolis of perhaps 2,000. In less than a mile, you're out of town and on a country road that winds through farms and crosses a gentle stream. For several miles you'll see typical farmland. Then, after you go through the town of Arendtsville, you'll enter serious orchard territory. These orchards are a breathtaking sight when all the trees are in bloom. As you ride, you'll see a mountain looming to the west, but you'll never have to climb it. The ride stays in the valley.

In addition to the cultivated fruits, you'll also find wild raspberries all along the ride. The black ones ripen first, in late June and

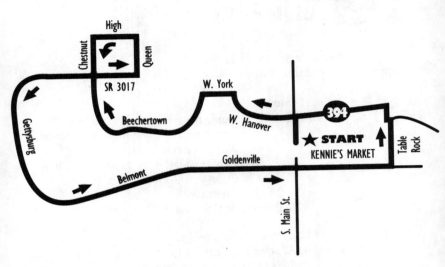

HOW to get there Biglerville is 8 miles north of Gettysburg and 30 miles south of Carlisle on Route 34. Gettysburg is on U.S. Route 30. Carlisle is on Interstate 81. To reach the start of the ride at Kennie's Market in Biglerville, follow Route 34 about 2 blocks south of the main intersection in town.

DIRECTIONS for the ride

- Leave the Kennie's Market parking lot and go north (right) on Main Street (Route 34).
- Left onto West Hanover Street (Route 394 west) at 0.2 mile.
- Left onto West York Street (Route 234 west) at 0.7 mile.
- Left onto Beecherstown Road at 0.9 mile.
- Right onto Gettysburg Street (SR 3017) at 4.1 miles.
- Left onto Queen Street at 4.7 miles.
- Left onto High Street at 4.8 miles.
- Left onto Chestnut Street at 5.3 miles.
- Right onto Gettysburg Street at 5.4 miles.
- Left onto Belmost Road at 9.7 miles.
- Right onto Goldenville Road at 11.4 miles.
- Cross Route 34 at 12.3 miles.
- Left onto Table Rock Road at 12.9 miles.
- Straight onto Route 394 west at stop sign at 14.6 miles.
- Left onto South Main Street at 16.7 miles.
- Return to Kennie's at 17.0 miles.

early July. The red ones appear around the middle of July. Cherries begin to ripen in the middle of June; peaches, pears, and apples toward the end of July. Different varieties come into their prime all the way through October.

This is a ride without any major tourist attractions along the way. Just off the route, however, is the site of the Apple Blossom Festival (early April) and Apple Harvest Festival (first two weekends in October). These take place at South Mountain Fairgrounds on Route 34 west of Arendtsville. The fairgrounds are easy to reach. When the ride directions indicate a left turn on High Street in Arendtsville, go right instead. You'll see the fairgrounds about 2 miles down on Route 34 north.

As a whole this ride is scenic and and low on traffic. The closest ride is Gettysburg, which is about 8 miles south on Route 34.

Carlisle

Number of miles:	17.5
Approximate pedaling time:	1¼ hours
Terrain:	Flat
Surface:	Good
Things to see:	Scenic farmlands, Trout Art Gallery at Dickinson College, U.S. Army War College
Food:	Restaurants at start of ride and in downtown Carlisle
Facilities:	At beginning and end of ride

On this ride you'll have several opportunities to put your bike into its highest gear and see how fast you can go. There are four sections of country roads that are at least 2 miles long and very short on hills and traffic.

When you start riding, don't be surprised if you feel a surge of athletic ability. This is an area that has produced an unusual number of outstanding athletes. The most famous was Jim Thorpe, the famed Olympian who won gold medals in the pentathlon and decathlon in the 1912 games. Before that he was a star player at the Carlisle Indian School, which today is part of the U.S. Army War College. In more recent years Carlisle High School has produced basketball player Billy Owens and baseball player Sid Bream. In July and August Dickinson College hosts the summer training camp of the Washington Redskins.

Carlisle also has a lot of history behind it. It was the home of two signers of the Declaration of Independence, James Wilson and George Ross. On the square in town is the First Presbyterian Church, built in 1757. Here the citizens chose Wilson and Ross as their representa-

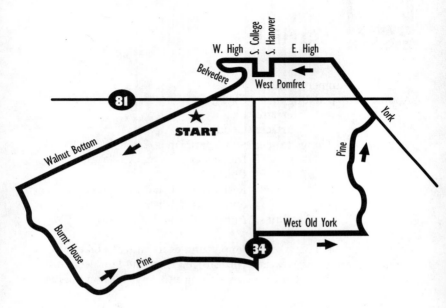

HOW to get there Take Interstate 81 to Exit 13; the ride begins at the McDonald's there. Carlisle can also be reached by Pennsylvania Routes 34 and 641 and by U.S Route 11.

DIREC-TIONS for the ride

- Leave McDonald's and go right on Walnut Bottom Road.
- Left onto Burnt House Road at 3.1 miles.
- Left onto Pine Road at 6.1 miles.
- Left onto Route 34 north at 7.6 miles (be careful).
- Right onto West Old York Road (Route 174 east) at 8.3 miles.
- Left onto Pine Road at 10.5 miles.
- Left onto York Road at 13.6 miles.
- Left onto East High Street (Route 641 west) at 14.3 miles.
- Left onto South Hanover Street at 14.8 miles.
- Right onto West Pomeret Street at 15.1 miles.
- Right onto South College Avenue at 15.5 miles.
- Left onto West High Street at 15.6 miles.
- Left onto Belvedere at 16.0 miles.
- Right onto Walnut Bottom at 17.0 miles.
- Finish at McDonald's at 17.5 miles.

tives in the Continental Congress. In 1863 a Civil War battle took place here, but the action in nearby Gettysburg was much more ferocious and gained much more fame. Carlisle was also the home of the last American manufacturer of bicycle tires.

As you ride you'll see a mountain looming just a few miles away, but you'll never have to climb it. The ride has no serious climbs. When you get into Carlisle, you'll find a nice small town, and you'll ride around Dickinson College. Signs point the way to the Army War College, the Cumberland County Historical Society, and the Trout Art Gallery.

Gettysburg

Number of miles:	17
Approximate pedaling time:	2 hours
Terrain:	Rolling, several good hills
Surface:	Good
Things to see:	Gettysburg Battlefield, Eisenhower Farm
Food:	Many restaurants near start and finish of ride; several on Howard Avenue, near 14-mile mark on tour
Facilities:	At Visitor Center and several places on battlefield

From July 1 to July 3, 1863, the small Pennsylvania town of Gettysburg gained lasting fame. During those three days of the Civil War, the bloodiest battle in the history of North America raged over farm fields and through the town. On November 18, 1863, President Abraham Lincoln delivered his famous Gettysburg Address here. Today the Gettysburg National Military Park offers a great opportunity to bicycle through history.

Many parts of the battlefield are almost the same today as they were on the evening of July 3, 1863. Fences, cannons, and rocks have not been moved. But there have been many additions: monuments, observation towers, and educational displays.

The ride is a very pretty one. The fields are green and surrounded by woodlands. In the spring, the pink blossoms of the dogwood trees, the yellow of the dandelions, and the violet of the violets turn the battlefield into a blaze of color. And while this was briefly a battlefield, today there's a powerful feeling of serenity in the air.

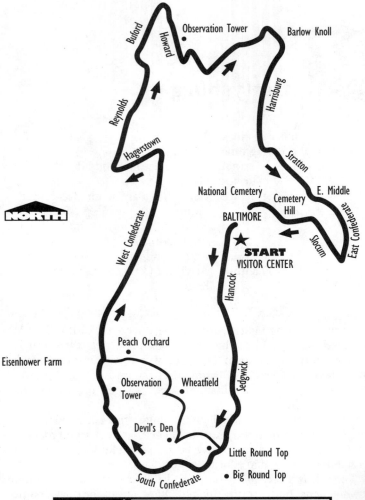

Buford
Howard
Observation Tower
Barlow Knoll
Harrisburg
Reynolds
Hagerstown
Stratton
National Cemetery
E. Middle
Cemetery Hill
BALTIMORE
East Confederate
NORTH
West Confederate
★ START
VISITOR CENTER
Slocum
Hancock
Peach Orchard
Eisenhower Farm
Observation Tower
Wheatfield
Sedgwick
Devil's Den
Little Round Top
Big Round Top
South Confederate

HOW to get there
Gettysburg lies at the intersections of U.S. Routes 30 and 15 and at the intersection of U.S. 30 and Route 34. The Gettysburg Visitor Center is just south of the town square on Baltimore Avenue.

DIREC-TIONS for the ride

The best method is to follow the signs. They'll guide you all around the battlefield.

- Leaving the Visitor Center, go right onto Hancock Avenue.
- Hancock becomes Sedgwick.
- Right onto South Confederate Avenue.
- South Confederate becomes West Confederate.
- Left onto Hagerstown Road.
- Left onto Reynolds Avenue.
- Reynolds becomes Buford Avenue.
- Right onto Howard Avenue.
- Right onto Harrisburg Road.
- Harrisburg Road becomes Stratton Street.
- Left onto East Middle Street.
- Right onto East Confederate Avenue.
- Right onto Slocum Avenue.
- Right onto Baltimore Street.
- Return to Visitor Center.

At the park Visitor Center you can see exhibits and mementos and pick up a brochure that will guide you on your tour. There are tours listed for cars and for bikes. The auto tour is better; it's 17 miles and it covers the entire battlefield. The bike tour is only about 6 miles.

The first stop on the tour is the High Water Mark. It was here that Union soldiers stopped the advance of General George E. Pickett and his troops. This effectively ended the Battle of Gettysburg and sent the Confederates into retreat.

As you continue on Hancock Avenue, you'll come to the Pennsylvania Memorial. This monument pays tribute to the 35,000 Pennsylvanians who fought here. Hancock turns into Sedgwick Avenue, which turns into Confederate Avenue. There are signs all along the way. The best view is available at Little Round Top. From here, you can get a look at much of the battle area.

The Eisenhower Farm, home of former President Dwight Eisenhower, is just west of Confederate Avenue, but they won't let you bike through it. It's accessible only by shuttle buses that leave from the Visitor Center.

On West Confederate Avenue is an observation tower that you can climb for a great view of the area. There's also a tower close to the Visitor Center. It's bigger but it costs money. The one on West Confederate is free.

Throughout this ride be wary of cars. They generally move slowly, but often the drivers are looking at the monuments instead of the road. Allow plenty of time for the ride. You'll probably want to stop and look frequently.

Newport

Number of miles:	17
Approximate pedaling time:	1½ hours
Terrain:	One good hill, otherwise flat to rolling
Surface:	Good
Things to see:	Little Buffalo State Park, trees, streams, birds, animals
Food:	General store (4.5 miles); restaurants and stores in Newport
Facilities:	At Little Buffalo State Park, general store, and various places in Newport

If you love nightlife and crowds of people, you'll feel lost on this ride. There are probably more people living on some blocks in New York City than there are in all of Perry County. And although Perry County comes within a mile of Harrisburg, it has remained rural and unspoiled. In fact, the county still doesn't have a traffic light. Most of the region is still forest, with some farms mixed in.

Little Buffalo State Park offers all sorts of outdoor activities—camping, swimming, boating, and hiking . The ride begins there and heads west on Little Buffalo Creek Road. The road is relatively flat, although the hills rise steeply beside it. The only tough hill on the ride comes after you go right on SR 4005 at about 3½ miles. You'll have a decent climb, then you'll drop down into a valley and meander along a creek.

The big town on the ride is Newport. This is the kind of place where neighbors know one another and you can walk from one end of the shopping district to the other in about five minutes. The main road into town is U.S. Route 322/22. This is a road that owes its four-

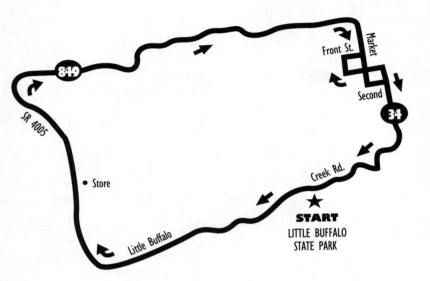

NORTH

849

SR 4005

Front St.

Market

Second

34

Creek Rd.

• Store

★ **START**
**LITTLE BUFFALO
STATE PARK**

Little Buffalo

HOW
to get
there
Little Buffalo State Park, where the ride
begins, is on Little Buffalo Creek Road,
about 2 miles west of Route 34, just south
of Newport. To get to Newport, take U.S.
Route 322/22 out of Harrisburg. Then go south
on Route 34 and look for signs for Little Buffalo
State Park.

DIREC-TIONS
for the ride

- Leave the Park Office at Little Buffalo State Park and go west on Little Buffalo Creek Road.
- Right (toward Skyline Corner General Store) onto SR 4005 at end of Little Buffalo Creek Road.
- Straight through intersection at 4.5 miles.
- Right onto Route 849 east at 5.9 miles.
- Left onto Market Street at 13.2 miles
- Left onto Second Street at 13.3 miles
- Right onto unnamed street at 13.6 miles (look for baseball fields).
- Right onto Front Street at 13.7 miles.
- Right onto Market Street at 13.9 miles.
- Left onto Second Street (Route 34 south) at 14.0 miles.
- Right onto Little Buffalo Creek Road at 15.0 miles (signs to park).
- Right to Park Office at 17.0 miles.

lane status to Penn State football. Although politicians may argue otherwise, the road was improved in order to carry fans from the eastern half of the state to State College. When the Nittany Lions aren't playing, there's not a lot of traffic out on the highway. It's also one of the prettiest roads anywhere, as its two-tier construction affords great views of the Juniata (not Juanita) River.

This is a great ride for getting away from it all. It's very pretty and very quiet. If you come in the autumn, it's really spectacular. If you're interested in a longer ride, stop at the office at Little Buffalo State Park. They have maps of the county, and they can tell you what's out there besides trees.

Thompsontown

Number of miles:	26.3
Approximate pedaling time:	2½ hours
Terrain:	Almost flat
Surface:	Good
Things to see:	Forests, farms, trains, Juniata River, small towns
Food:	In Thompsontown, Port Royal, Mexico, and Mifflintown
Facilities:	At beginning, and in towns

The Juniata River is the major waterway through south central Pennsylvania. This ride takes you for a scenic, low-traffic ride through the Juniata River Valley, on both sides of the river. By Pennsylvania standards, it's flat.

Juniata County is lightly populated, because most of the area is quite mountainous. On this ride you'll have steep hillsides looming around you, but you won't have to climb any of them. As you begin, you'll cross the Juniata River, and you'll see railroad tracks. They're the main east-west tracks for Amtrak and Conrail, so rail fans will want to bring along a camera.

Most of the first 10 miles are through a forest where wildlife is abundant. Don't be surprised to see deer, turkey vultures, bluebirds, foxes, and maybe even a bear. They've been moving back into the area, but they pose no threat to humans, unless the humans threaten them.

When the forest ends, you'll come into several small towns, the first of which is Port Royal. Its fame comes from its auto-racing track, which operates on weekends in warm weather. Mifflin and Mif-

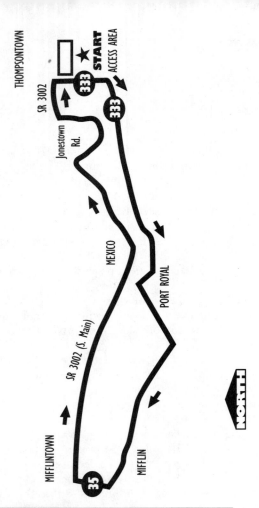

THOMPSONTOWN

START
★
ACCESS AREA

333

333

SR 3002

Jonestown Rd.

MEXICO

PORT ROYAL

SR 3002 (S. Main)

MIFFLINTOWN

MIFFLIN

35

NORTH

HOW to get there
Thompsontown is on U.S. 322, about 40 miles west of Harrisburg. Take the exit for Route 333. Follow 333 west to the Fish Commission Access beside the Juniata River.

DIRECTIONS for the ride

- Leave the access area and go left, across the river.
- Follow Route 333 West to Mifflin.
- Take Route 35 North across the river at 14.1 miles.
- Right onto South Main Street (SR 3002) at 14.7 miles.
- Right onto Jonestown Road at 21.0 miles.
- Right onto SR 3002 at 23.6 miles.
- Right onto Route 333 at 25.6 miles.
- Finish at 26.3 miles.

---

flintown are small towns on either side of the river. Mexico is an even smaller town.

After you pass Port Royal, you'll move into farm country. On the north side of the river, farms, many owned by Amish families, are quite common. Like most Pennsylvania rides, this one can be especially spectacular in October, when the leaves are changing.

Bloomsburg

Number of miles:	12
Approximate pedaling time:	1 hour
Terrain:	Downhill at beginning, uphill at end, flat for middle 8 miles
Surface:	Good, but be careful going over covered bridge
Things to see:	Bloomsburg University, Bloomsburg Fair, small college town
Food:	Many places in town; also at beginning of ride
Facilities:	At Bloomsburg Town Park; also in many places in town

Situated along the Susquehanna River in northern Pennsylvania, Bloomsburg is a college town surrounded by a rich agricultural area. It's also home to several large textile mills. In addition, Bloomsburg has the distinction of being the only incorporated town in the state. By a quirk of the language, all other developed areas in Pennsylvania are cities, boroughs, or villages. (And, in fact, the state itself is officially a commonwealth, one of four in the United States.)

This ride starts at Bloomsburg's Tourist Information Center and spends most of its miles in the town, taking you past the Fairgrounds and the university and through the center of town. But the streets are wide and pleasant. The downtown has been restored, and part of it is a National Historic District.

The first 2 miles of the route give you a great downhill ride to Bloomsburg proper. When you reach Railroad Avenue, you'll see the Fairgrounds. In rural Pennsylvania communities fairs are big business and big fun. During the last week in September, Bloomsburg is home

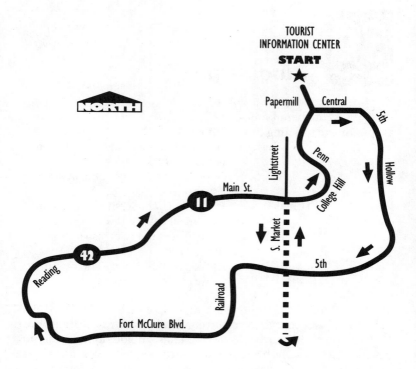

NORTH

TOURIST
INFORMATION CENTER
START

Papermill   Central   5th

Lightstreet   Penn   Hollow

Main St.   College Hill

S. Market   5th

Reading   Railroad

Fort McClure Blvd.

HOW to get there   Take Interstate 80 to Exit 35 and follow signs to Tourist Information Center, where the ride begins. Or take U.S. Route 11 into Bloomsburg and go north on Route 487, Lightstreet Road, to Tourist Information Center.

DIREC-TIONS for the ride

- Begin at Tourist Information Center at Exit 35 of Interstate 80. Go left on Papermill Road out of parking lot and cross Route 487 (Lightstreet Road) onto Central Road.
- Right onto 5th/Hollow Road at 0.2 mile.
- Left onto Railroad Street at 3.1 miles.
- Right onto Fort McClure Boulevard at 3.9 miles.
- Right onto Reading Street (first right after covered bridge) at 5.6 miles.
- Right onto Route 42 at 5.9 miles.
- Left onto U.S. Route 11 at 6.6 miles.
- Right onto South Market Street at 7.8 miles.
- Return to Main Street.
- Right onto Main Street at 9.8 miles.
- Straight ahead, up College Hill at 10.1 miles.
- Left onto Penn Street at 10.2 miles.
- Right onto Lightstreet Road at 10.3 miles.
- Left onto Papermill Road at 12.2 miles.
- Right to Tourist Information Center.

to one of Pennsylvania's biggest fairs. It features agricultural and industrial exhibits, rides, food, and big-name entertainers. Thousands of visitors pour into town, partly for the activities but mostly for the food.

Past the Fairgrounds, turn onto Fort McClure Boulevard. Behind the trees on your left is the Susquehanna River. After a mile and a half on this road, you'll come to a covered bridge. Then you'll pick up the main road into the heart of town.

At the bottom of Market Street is the Bloomsburg Town Park. This is a good place to stop to eat, relax, and watch the river flow. As you start up the hill that leads out of town, you'll see Bloomsburg University, a state-supported university. From there, it's back to the Tourist Information Center.

If you can swing it, the ideal time to do this ride is a September Saturday when the Bloomsburg Huskies football team is playing at home and the Bloomsburg Fair is going on across town.

Eagles Mere

Number of miles:	14
Approximate pedaling time:	1½ hours
Terrain:	Very hilly
Surface:	Good
Things to see:	Resort town of Eagles Mere, Eagles Mere Lake, Sullivan County Museum (open Wednesday afternoons and Saturdays)
Food:	In Laporte and Eagles Mere
Facilities:	In Laporte and Eagles Mere

Eagles Mere is a tiny town that's a summer home for many families. It's like a beach resort, except that it's situated on top of a mountain and it has a lake instead of an ocean.

The area surrounding Eagles Mere is known as The Endless Mountains, and the description is apt. This ride includes a couple of tough climbs and also a couple of great downhill runs.

The ride begins in Laporte, the county seat of Sullivan County, the least densely populated county in eastern Pennsylvania. In Laporte you'll find a general store, the county courthouse, a lot of trees, and a green with park benches. The road from Laporte to Eagles Mere passes through almost unbroken woodlands. There are a few houses, but it's mostly trees.

On the edge of Eagles Mere is a sign that proclaims its elevation—2,126 feet. The elevation and the lake have combined to make the town a summer resort. The elevation makes Eagles Mere cooler than most parts of the state, and the lake is the focus of summer activities such as swimming and boating. In winter the lake freezes and becomes a popular spot for ice and snow activities.

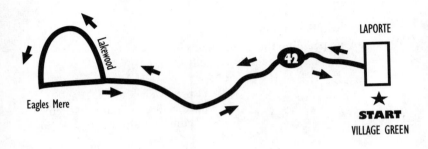

LAPORTE

Eagles Mere

Lakewood

42

★
START
VILLAGE GREEN

HOW to get there
Laporte is on US 220, between Williamsport and Towanda. Eagles Mere is on Route 42.

**DIREC-
TIONS**
for the ride

- Start in Laporte at the courthouse, at the intersection of Muncy and Main.
- Go south on Route 42.
- Right onto Lakewood at 5.2 miles.
- Left onto Eagles Mere Avenue (Route 42) at 7.2 miles.
- Finish at 14.0 miles.

Eagles Mere has a number of shops, which offer antiques, books, and ice cream, designed to attract tourists. It also has several inns, in case you'd like to stay overnight. On a clear day you can get a great view of the valley to the south.

Back in Laporte you can check out local history at the Sullivan County Museum, which is just behind the courthouse.

Eckley

Number of miles:	10.1
Approximate pedaling time:	1 hour
Terrain:	Rolling, no tough hills
Surface:	Fair
Things to see:	Eckley Miners Village, coal-mining museum, strip mines, town of Freeland
Food:	In Freeland
Facilities:	At museum, and in Freeland

Coal was the attraction that brought thousands of European immigrants to northeastern Pennsylvania during the 19th and early 20th centuries. They came to work in the mines and found jobs that were dangerous and dirty. At Eckley you can get a glimpse of life in a mining town. Movie watchers saw Eckley in *The Molly Maguires*, which was filmed here.

Eckley is a *patch* town that's less than a mile long. In its prime, the mining company owned everthing—the mines, houses, stores, hotel, and schools. Underground mining operations began around 1854, and the population of Eckley peaked in 1870 at more than 1,000. Strip mining began in 1890, and the work force and general population gradually declined. That scenario has recurred across the entire region. Pennsylvania's coal production peaked in the 1920s and has been declining since because other fuels are cleaner and easier to obtain. Around Eckley, however, some mining still goes on, and you'll be able to see several strip mines as you ride.

Today, the museum at Eckley depicts the lives of coal miners in the town and across *the coal regions,* which is how Pennsylvanians

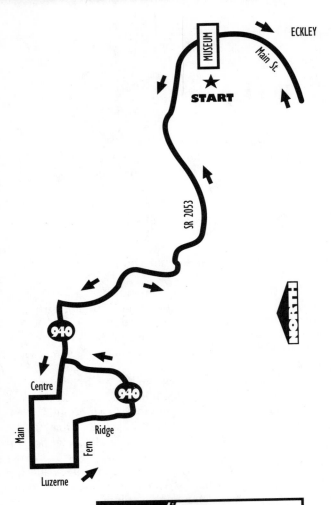

ECKLEY

Main St.

MUSEUM

★
START

SR 2053

NORTH

940

Centre

940

Main

Ridge

Fern

Luzerne

HOW to get there   Take Route 940 East from Hazelton or West from I-80 and follow signs for Eckley Miners Village.

**DIREC-
TIONS
for the ride**

- Leave the museum and go left on SR 2053.
- Left onto Route 940 at 3.1 miles.
- Right onto Centre Street at 3.5 miles.
- Left onto Main Street at 3.6 miles.
- Left onto Fern Street at 3.8 miles.
- Left onto Luzerne Street at 3.9 miles.
- Right onto Ridge Street at 4.0 miles.
- Left at T-intersection (Route 940) at 4.3 miles.
- Right onto Route 940 at 4.6 miles.
- Right onto SR 2053 at 5.1 miles.
- Right into museum at 8.3 miles.

Note: The village is about .9 mile long. If you ride to the end and back, you'll have traveled 10.1 miles.

refer to a large area of their state. In fact, Pennsylvania produces two different types of coal. Bituminous, or soft coal, is more common. Anthracite, which comes out of the ground at Eckley, is harder, and it burns more cleanly.

The ride begins at the museum and goes to the small town of Freeland. The entire area sits on top of a mountain, so there are no especially strenuous climbs. Along the route you can see coal mines that are still operating. You'll also see some amazing sights where grass and trees have somehow managed to grow in the residue left from the mining and refining process.

Honesdale

Number of miles: 11.7
Approximate pedaling time: 1 hour
Terrain: Hilly
Surface: Fair
Things to see: America's first railroad, Wayne County fairgrounds, Wayne County Museum
Food: In Honesdale
Facilities: In Honesdale

Honesdale is a pretty little town in the Pocono Mountains of Wayne County. It lies in a basin, surrounded on all sides by fairly steep hills, and, while it's the biggest town in the county, it's definately a small town. The village green, across from the courthouse, is a pleasant place to sit and relax after your ride.

In 1829 Honesdale became the site of the first trip by steam locomotive in the United States, when the Stourbridge Lion made its initial journey. Imported from England to haul coal from nearby mines to the Delaware and Hudson Canal, it proved too heavy for the rails. Despite that early disappointment, trains played a big part in Honesdale's growth. Today, the town's rail heritage is still strong. During the summer and fall, and near holidays such as Easter, Halloween, and Christmas, weekend excursion trains run from Honesdale to Hawley and Lackawaxen.

If your travel around Pennsylvania, you'll observe that, to a considerable extent, Wayne County reverses traditional land-use patterns. In many places farms are in the valleys, while the higher areas remain unpopulated. In Wayne County, however, many farms are on the tops of hills, and the lowlands are home to the area's towns.

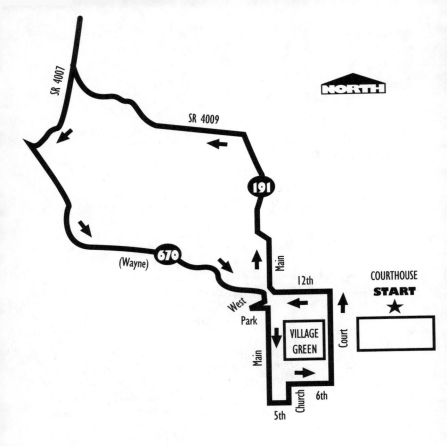

SR 4007

SR 4009

191

670 (Wayne)

Main

12th

West

Park

VILLAGE GREEN

Main

Court

Church

6th

5th

COURTHOUSE

START ★

NORTH

HOW to get there   Honesdale is in the northeastern corner of Pennsylvania, at the intersection of U.S. 6, Route 191, and Route 670. From I-84, take Route 191 North. From I-81, take U.S. 6 East.

- Begin at the Wayne County Court House, two blocks east of Main Street, and go north on Court Street.
- Left onto 12th Street at 0.2 mile.
- Right onto Main Street at 0.3 mile.
- North onto Route 191.
- Left onto SR 4009 at 4.2 miles.
- Left onto SR 4007 at 5.7 miles.
- Left onto Wayne Street (Route 670) at 6.9 miles.
- Right onto Main Street at 9.9 miles.
- Right onto West Street at 10.1 miles.
- Left onto Park Street at 10.5 miles.
- Right onto Main Street at 10.6 miles.
- Train rides are at 10.8 miles.
- Left onto Fifth Street at 11.2 miles.
- Left onto Church Street at 11.3 miles.
- Right onto Sixth Street at 11.35 miles.
- Left onto Court Street at 11.4 miles.
- Finish at 11.7 miles.

Agriculture and logging are both important here, and they're on display at The Wayne County Fair. It takes place in early August at the fairgrounds on Route 191, about a mile and a half into the ride.

Jim Thorpe

Number of miles:	18
Approximate pedaling time:	1¾ hours
Terrain:	Mountainous
Surface:	Good
Things to see:	Town of Jim Thorpe, Packer mansions, Mauch Chunk Lake Park, whitewater rafting on Lehigh River, Jim Thorpe Memorial
Food:	In downtown Jim Thorpe and at several places along route
Facilities:	At Mauch Chunk Lake Park and Nesquehoning

Located in the Pocono Mountains, Jim Thorpe acquired its name in the 1950s when two small towns, Mauch Chunk and East Mauch Chunk, joined forces and incorporated as Jim Thorpe in order to give one of America's great athletes a fitting burial place.

In its early days Mauch Chunk was a center for canal boats that hauled coal down the Lehigh Canal. Later, Asa Packer built the Lehigh Valley Railroad from Mauch Chunk to Aston. Today this scenic little town, sometimes called "the Switzerland of America," draws many visitors. Some come just to look, but many come for active outings.

The lookers can enjoy a museum, gift shops, mansions, and the burial place of Jim Thorpe. The active visitor can swim, hike, raft, and bike.

This ride is not for the faint of heart or the weak of quadriceps. Jim Thorpe sits at the bottom of a valley, right beside the Lehigh

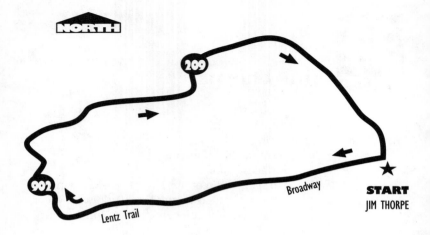

NORTH

209

902

Lentz Trail

Broadway

★
START
JIM THORPE

HOW to get there   Jim Thorpe is on U.S. Route 209 in northeastern Pennsylvania. Take the Northeast Extension of the Pennsylvania Turnpike to Exit 34 and pick up 209 south there. The railroad station is on Route 209, in the downtown district, at the traffic light. It houses the Visitor Center.

DIRECTIONS for the ride

- Start at the railroad station (Visitor Center) downtown.
- West (uphill) on Broadway. Look for signs pointing to Mauch Chunk Lake Park.
- Broadway becomes Lentz Trail.
- Right onto Route 902 west at 7.0 miles.
- Right onto U.S. Route 209 north at 9.3 miles.
- Finish at 17.7 miles.

River, and there's only one way out—up. In fact, Jim Thorpe's topography is typical of many towns in Pennsylvania.

When you leave Jim Thorpe, it's four miles to Mauch Chunk Lake Park. Here you can swim, hike, eat, or camp. Past the park you'll come to the towns of Summit Hill and Nesquehoning. Once you reach Summit Hill, it's almost all downhill. It's a fast ride from there back to Jim Thorpe.

This is an area that's quite popular with mountain-bike enthusiasts. There are old logging and mining trails on many of the nearby hillsides, and every year a big gathering of mountain bikers takes place here. There's also a triathlon in July that starts at Mauch Chunk Lake Park and features a wild bike ride from there to downtown.

Incidentally, *Mauch Chunk* means "sleeping bear."

Washingtonville

Number of miles:	19
Approximate pedaling time:	1½ hours
Terrain:	Flat, one hill
Surface:	Good
Things to see:	Montour Preserve, fertile farmlands
Food:	In Washingtonville, store at 8.4 miles
Facilities:	At Montour Preserve

This ride is amazingly flat. In 19 miles you'll have only one hill. It's also a very pretty ride, meandering through some of the best farmland in north central Pennsylvania.

The ride begins at the Montour Preserve. The Preserve, maintained by the Pennsylvania Power and Light Company (PP&L), is a great place to see nature at work. It offers picnic areas, Lake Chillisquaque for boating, hiking trails, Wildlife Management areas, and even a fossil pit where you can dig and keep whatever you find.

The Laura Smith Trail of History will take you through the Preserve. If you follow this trail, you can see old farmhouses, farm tools, barns, and the little Chillisquaque Creek.

Leaving the Preserve, you'll ride out into the farm country of Montour County. On the roads you'll probably see some Amish horses and buggies. The ride goes through a lush valley nestled between the Muncy Hills to the north and the Montour Ridge to the south. You'll see steep hills looming around you, but except for the little climb at 8.5 miles, you won't have to go up any of them. The major town on the ride is Washingtonville, a quiet little farming community.

You'll see two big towers as you ride. They are part of the Montour Steam Electric Station, a coal-fired generating plant operated by PP&L to supply electricity for Pennsylvania.

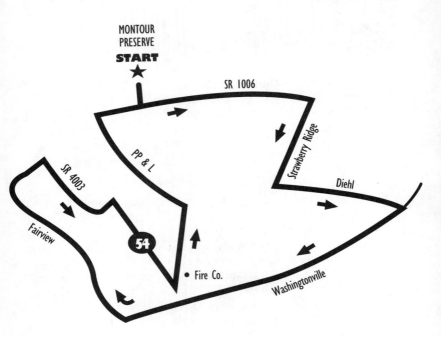

HOW to get there The Montour Preserve, where your ride begins, lies close to Route 54 in Montour County, north of Interstate 80 and Washingtonville. Get off Interstate 80 at Exit 33 and go north on Route 54. The signs will direct you to the Preserve.

DIREC-TIONS for the ride

- Leave the parking lot at the Montour Preserve and go left on SR 1006.
- Right onto Strawberry Ridge Road (SR 1002) at 1.7 miles.
- Left onto Diehl Road at 3.7 miles.
- Right onto Washingtonville Road at 5.2 miles.
- Right onto Fairview Road at 8.4 miles.
- Right onto SR 4003 at 11.2 miles (stop sign).
- Right onto Route 54 at 12.3 miles.
- Left onto unmarked road at 15.0 miles. Look for signs to Montour Preserve and Washingtonville Volunteer Fire Company.
- Left onto PP&L Road at 16.0 miles.
- Left into Preserve at 19.2 miles.

Notice the farms in this valley. PP&L owns some of them and leases them to local farmers, stipulating that they employ modern farming practices such as crop rotation, contour farming, and erosion control. The results of excellent land management are increased yields and better soil fertility. In this verdant valley man and nature do a great job of getting along.

Loganton/Sugar Valley

Number of miles:	15.4
Approximate pedaling time:	1½ hours
Terrain:	Almost flat
Surface:	Good
Things to see:	Small town, covered bridge, fertile valley
Food:	In Loganton
Facilities:	In Loganton

The dictionary defines a valley as "a stretch of low land lying between hills or mountains and usually having a stream or river flowing through it." Sugar Valley fits that definition perfectly.

Sugar Valley is about 1 mile wide and 10 miles long. It lies just south of I-80, but most of the traffic zooms by, never stopping to investigate what lies nearby.

Steep hillsides rise on both sides of the valley. Fishing Creek runs right down the middle, and most of the land in the valley is farmed. For a bicyclist it's a great place to take a leisurely ride. There are only a few roads in the valley, but they don't have much traffic on them. And many residents of the valley are Amish farmers, who use buggies instead of cars.

Loganton is a picturesque small town. It's home to the valley's schools and a few businesses. Once you get out of town, you're immediately in farm country. On Logan's Mill Road you'll pass through Logan's Mill Bridge, the only covered bridge left in Clinton County. After a short climb away from the water, you'll be on the south side of the valley. From there you'll have an excellent view of the valley's farms and orchards.

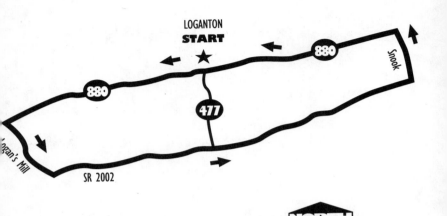

LOGANTON
START

880

477

880

Snook

Logan's Mill

SR 2002

NORTH

HOW to get there
Loganton lies just south of I-80, about 30 miles west of the Susquehanna River. Follow the signs for Route 880.

DIREC-TIONS for the ride

- Begin in the center of Loganton, at the intersection of Route 880 and Route 477.
- Go south on 880.
- Left onto Logan's Mill Road at 5.5 miles.
- Left onto SR 2002 at 6.4 miles.
- Left onto Snook Road at 11.8 miles.
- Left onto Route 880 at 12.7 miles.
- Finish at 15.4 miles.

As rides go, this is short on tourist attractions but long on scenery and enjoyable riding.

Penn's Creek

Number of miles:	17
Approximate pedaling time:	1½ hours
Terrain:	Rolling
Surface:	Mostly good; one bad stretch on School Road
Things to see:	Walnut Acres Organic Farm, rolling farmlands, Buggy Museum
Food:	At Walnut Acres and in Mifflinburg and New Berlin
Facilities:	At Walnut Acres and in Mifflinburg and New Berlin

This pleasant jaunt will take you through the fertile farmlands of Union and Snyder counties. Beginning at Walnut Acres Farm, you'll pass farm after farm and go through two small towns.

Walnut Acres Farm was one of the first in the country to make the break from chemical farming. In 1946, long before organic foods gained the popularity that they have today, Paul Keene decided to grow his crops without applying harmful chemicals to the land. Today, Mr. Keene is still active in his business, and Walnut Acres is a big food company. (Well, big by the standards of its industry, although still small in comparison to a company such as Kraft or Hershey's.)

At Walnut Acres you'll find a retail store and a small restaurant. Actually, a very small percentage of Walnut Acres' sales come from this store. Most of their sales come through natural-food stores and mail order. You can also take plant tours. If you're really lucky, you'll get there on a day when they're roasting peanuts and making peanut butter.

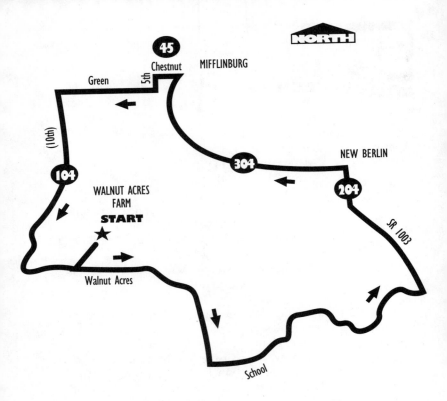

NORTH

45 Chestnut MIFFLINBURG

Green

5th

(10th)

104

WALNUT ACRES
FARM

START
★

Walnut Acres

304

NEW BERLIN

204

SR 1003

School

HOW
to get
there

From Harrisburg, take U.S. Route 15
north to Route 104 north. Go about 20
miles and look for the signs for Walnut
Acres; the ride begins at Walnut Acres Farm.
From Lewisburg, take Route 45 west to 104
south and look for the Walnut Acres signs.

DIRECTIONS for the ride

- Leave Walnut Acres Farm and turn right on Walnut Acres Road.
- Left onto School Road at 1.7 miles.
- Left onto SR 1003 at 4.7 miles.
- Left onto Route 204 north at 6.3 miles (New Berlin).
- Left onto Chestnut Street (Route 45 West) at 12.1 miles (Mifflinburg).
- Left onto 5th Street at 12.2 miles.
- Right onto Green Street at 12.3 miles.
- Left onto 10th Street (Route 104 south) at 12.8 miles.
- Left onto Walnut Acres Road at 16.4 miles.
- Right into Walnut Acres Farm at 17.0 miles.

When you head out on the roads, you'll be in farm country. The first town that you'll reach is New Berlin, a quiet town with a nice little park right beside the creek.

Five miles down the road from New Berlin, you'll come to Mifflinburg, the biggest town on the ride. Mifflinburg offers several places of interest. One is the Buggy Museum. At one time, Mifflinburg was the carriage-making center of the world. The museum remembers those days. And on Chestnut Street you'll find a quilt shop that features quilts made by the Amish and Mennonite ladies of the area.

TURKEY PATH

THE TURKEY PATH WINDS 1 MILE TO THE
CANYON FLOOR AND PARALLELS LITTLE
FOUR MILE RUN FOR ABOUT HALF ITS LENGTH.
FOREST LIFE, GEOLOGY AND WATERFALLS
HIGHLIGHT THE 1.5 HOUR ROUND TRIP.

WARNING:

AS SECTIONS OF THIS TRAIL ARE NARROW,
STEEP AND HAZARDOUS; PROPER FOOTGEAR
SHOULD BE WORN.
THE TRAIL IS MARKED WITH ORANGE
BLAZES LIKE THIS:
PLEASE STAY ON MAIN TRAIL!

Wellsboro

Number of miles:	21.6 or 35
Approximate pedaling time:	2 or 3 hours
Terrain:	Hilly
Surface:	Fair
Things to See:	Town of Wellsboro, Pennsylvania Grand Canyon
Food:	In Wellsboro and at State Park
Facilities:	In Wellsboro and at State Park
Option:	Return via Route 6

Northern Pennsylvania is an area of small towns and great natural beauty. On this ride, you'll see both.

Wellsboro is a picture-postcard type of town. It features gaslit streets, a town green, and Victorian mansions. It's a pleasant and not very long walk from end to end. During June Wellsboro hosts the Pennsylvania State Laurel Festival. This is a street fair with food and entertainment, held to honor the mountain laurel, Pennsylvania's state flower, which grows both wild and cultivated all over the state. A major part of the Laurel Festival is a bike race of about 18 miles on the second Saturday in June.

Wellsboro's main claim to fame, however, is the Pennsylvania Grand Canyon. Located about 10 miles west of town, it's 50 miles long and 1,000 feet deep. Pine Creek flows rapidly along the bottom and attracts canoeists and kayakers.

Leonard Harrison State Park, the destination of the ride, is on the east rim of the canyon and offers spectacular views. It's also home to plenty of wildlife, even some bears. The Turkey Path is a series of switchbacks that take hikers down to the bottom of the canyon. It's a beautiful descent—and a good climb back to the top.

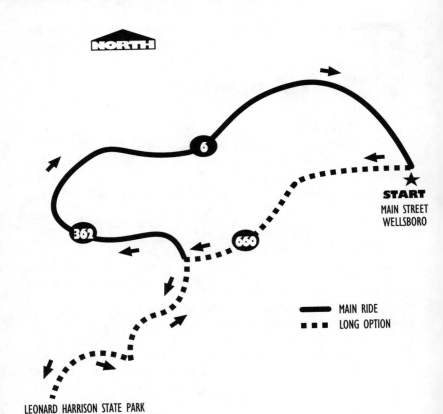

NORTH

6

362

660

★
START
MAIN STREET
WELLSBORO

——— MAIN RIDE
▪▪▪▪ LONG OPTION

LEONARD HARRISON STATE PARK
AND PENNSYLVANIA GRAND CANYON

HOW to get there
Wellsboro is on U.S. Route 6, which runs east and west across northern Pennsylvania. You can take U.S. Route 15 and exit onto Route 6 in Mansfield; then travel about 13 miles west to Wellsboro. Pennsylvania Routes 660 and 287 also run through Wellsboro.

- This one is very easy. Start at the Visitor Information Center, 120 Main Street, right in the center of Wellsboro, across from the green.
- Go west on Route 660 to Leonard Harrison State Park at 10.8 miles.
- Reverse your path and return to Wellsboro.

Optional variation

- When returning from State Park on Route 660, go left onto Route 362 west at 18.6 miles
- Right onto U.S. Route 6 east at 24 miles and return to Wellsboro Main Street.

The difference in elevation between the bottom and the top of the canyon is enough to create thermal updrafts. As you stand at the top, you'll probably be able to see birds soaring on the wind.

The ride climbs for the first few miles, then levels off and runs along the high ridges, through a largely agricultural area. There are some side roads, but unfortunately they're mostly gravel. If you have a mountain bike, this is a good place for it.

If you're looking for more bike routes in the area, stop in at the Wellsboro Visitor Information Center (where the ride begins). They have a pamphlet that outlines several rides around Tioga County.

Bicycle Rental Centers

Lancaster Bicycle Touring
3 Colt Ridge Lane
Strasburg, PA 17579
(717) 786–4492
(717) 394–8475
Touring and mountain bikes

New Horizons Bicycle Adventures
3495 Horizon Drive
Lancaster, PA 17601
(717) 285–7607
Mountain bikes

Pocono Whitewater Adventures
Pocono Inn-to-Inn Bicycle Tours
Route 903
Jim Thorpe, PA 18229
(717) 325–3665
Mountain bikes

Rasmussen Bike Rental
1 Boathouse Row (just west of the Museum of Art)
Philadelphia, PA 19104
(215) 978–8545

The Bike Peddler
205 Bridge Street
Phoenixville, PA 19453
(adjacent to Valley Forge)
(215) 783–2453

About the Author

Bill Simpson is a writer and an endurance-sport enthusiast. He lives in Lancaster, Pennsylvania, an area that he considers one of the great places in the world for biking. He has ridden tens of thousands of miles on his bike over Lancaster County's farm roads. His biking motto is "Nowhere to go and all day to get there." When he's not biking, he's often running. He has run more than thirty marathons, and his favorite is a Pennsylvania race, God's Country, through the mountains of Potter County. He is the author of *Guide to the Amish Country*.

Best Bike Rides
Short Bike Rides
Short Nature Walks

Here are the other fine titles offered in the **Best Bike Rides**, **Short Bike Rides**, and **Short Nature Walks** series, created for those who enjoy recreational cycling and nature walks. Please check your local bookstore for other Globe Pequot Press outdoor recreation titles.

The Best Bike Rides in New England, $12.95
The Best Bike Rides in the Pacific Northwest, $12.95
The Best Bike Rides in the South, $12.95
Short Bike Rides in and around Washington, D.C., $8.95
Short Bike Rides in Rhode Island, $8.95
Short Bike Rides Cape Cod, Nantucket, Vineyard, $8.95
Short Bike Rides in Connecticut, $8.95
Short Bike Rides in Long Island, $8.95
Short Bike Rides in New Jersey, $8.95
Short Bike Rides in and around New York City, $8.95
Short Nature Walks on Long Island, $8.95
Short Nature Walks Cape Cod and the Vineyard, $8.95
Sixty Selected Short Nature Walks in Connecticut, $8.95

To order any of these titles with MASTERCARD or VISA, call toll-free 1-800-243-0495; in Connecticut call 1-800-962-0973. Free shipping for orders of three or more books. Shipping charge of $3.00 per book for one or two books ordered. Connecticut residents add sales tax. Ask for free catalogue of Globe Pequot's quality books on recreation, travel, nature, gardening, cooking, crafts, and more. Prices subject to change.